AUDLEY END

CONTENTS

Published by English Heritage
Copyright © English Heritage 1997
First published 1997

Edited by Kate Jeffrey
Designed by Carroll Associates
Printed in England by The White Dove Press C100 3/97
ISBN 1 85074 642 7

Unless otherwise stated, all the photographs were taken by the English Heritage Photographic Unit
and remain the copyright of English Heritage.

Acknowledgements
English Heritage would like to thank Lord Braybrooke for the generous loan of many of the paintings, the silver
collection and other items, and also for his kind permission to reproduce photographs of many of the items.
We would also like to thank Mr (formerly Corporal) Peter Howe for sharing his wartime reminiscences of Audley End.
The Tryon Palace Historic Sites and Gardens, an agency of the North Carolina Department of Cultural Resources,
kindly allowed us to examine and copy for the Dining Parlour the rare turkey-pattern Axminster carpet in its collections.
In preparing this guidebook the authors have drawn extensively on the earlier English Heritage handbook
written by Paul Drury and Ian Gow.

Note to visitors
English Heritage is committed to preserving Audley End for future generations to enjoy, and asks for your help in achieving this.
Please respect the rules about not smoking or eating in the house, and refrain from touching any of the items on display.

INTRODUCTION

Richard Neville, third Lord Braybrooke (1783–1858) by John Hoppner

Audley End has a long and varied history in which episodes of spectacular building have been followed by periods of severe decline. This complex story is evident throughout the house: in the changing use of the rooms, the contrasting tastes in interiors, and the diverse collections of paintings and objects, all of which reflect the fluctuating family fortunes as well as the individual characters of the owners.

Originally one of the great Jacobean 'prodigy' houses, Audley End was built in 1603–14 by the first Earl of Suffolk with the express intention of providing accommodation for the visiting king, James I. Within four years of its completion, however, Suffolk had fallen from favour, and over the following centuries the house was gradually reduced and altered. In the second half of the eighteenth century Audley End was given a new lease of life by Sir John Griffin Griffin, who created an elegant suite of reception rooms with the help of the celebrated architect Robert Adam. Further enhancements were made to reflect Sir John's elevation to the peerage as Lord Howard de Walden in 1784.

Above all, however, the interiors that can be seen today represent the taste of the third Lord Braybrooke, who created a splendid sequence of first-floor reception rooms in the 1820s. The romantic 'Jacobean' character of these opulent rooms is a tribute to the third lord's antiquarian interest in the early history of his house.

The contents of the house tell a story in their own right. Sir John Griffin Griffin formed the basis of an ancestral picture collection, comprising family portraits and 'Old Master' paintings. This was augmented in the nineteenth century by paintings inherited through the Neville and Cornwallis families. The furniture and silver collections were similarly built up through a gradual process of inheritance and marriage.

In 1939 Audley End was requisitioned by the government, and during the Second World War it served as a secret training centre for the Polish section of the Special Operations Executive. The house was purchased for the nation in 1948 and is now in the care of English Heritage.

DISPLAY AND CONSERVATION

Today visitors follow a set route through the house. They begin in the formal open space of the Great Hall, then mount the stairs, as their nineteenth-century predecessors would have done, to the sequence of grand reception rooms created by the third Lord Braybrooke in the 1820s. Pausing to view Sir John Griffin Griffin's Gothick Chapel, they proceed through a series of family and guest rooms before descending by a different staircase. Back on the ground floor they see part of the nineteenth-century service area before finally visiting a fine suite of neoclassical reception rooms created by Robert Adam in the late eighteenth century.

From this synopsis an oddity immediately becomes apparent. Audley End has two sets of reception rooms, including a dining room and several drawing rooms each. Historically, these rooms did not coexist: the original Robert Adam suite was destroyed by the third Lord Braybrooke when he introduced his new sequence of reception rooms upstairs. The Adam rooms visitors see today are a recreation dating from the 1960s. Attitudes to historic houses have changed greatly in the last thirty years and today it is unlikely that the decision would be taken to recreate one period at the

Two aspects of presenting an historic house interior. BELOW *Reweaving an original silk tissue for display.* RIGHT *The careful conservation and cleaning of the interior of the Dolls' House*

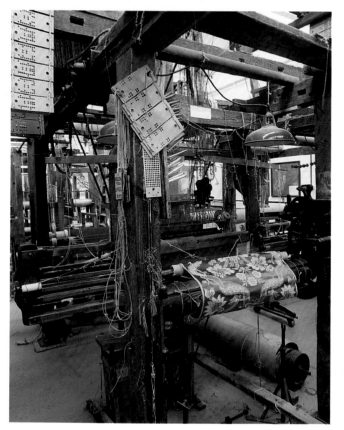

expense of preserving another. It is now considered more important to show how a house has evolved, giving an insight into changing tastes and patterns of use.

Regular visitors to country houses will appreciate that the interiors are dimly lit for conservation reasons, but should also be aware that the house would have appeared in a similar light throughout the period of family occupancy (electricity was first installed by the government during the Second World War). Pictures are hung in their historic locations, often densely arranged, illustrating the fact that the overall impression was considered at least as important as the individual works of art. Today the house is subject to far greater wear and tear from thousands of visitors than it once was from the families who often only used the rooms for part of the year. This has made it necessary to install stanchions and druggets to protect the historic carpets and furniture, and to request visitors not to touch fragile items.

Although museum standards of care and conservation are applied by English Heritage in preserving Audley End for future generations, and the house is no longer lived in, it still has a tale to tell. The interiors have both an historic and a social value, for they tell us how people lived here and how many of their aesthetic values have survived to the present day. Audley End continues to change and develop with each season as the work of conservation and presentation continues, enhancing a house that was, in the words of a nineteenth-century visitor, 'in perfect keeping in every part'.

A TOUR OF
AUDLEY END HOUSE

Please refer to the two floor plans on the inside back cover for the location of the rooms described in the tour.

1 ENTRANCE HALL

Visitors pass through the Jacobean porch, with its exuberant decoration, and into the house by way of the great oak door surmounted by an allegorical carving depicting the rewards of Peace.

Although the Entrance Hall is small and somewhat austere, it has served as one of the main entrances to Audley End since its construction in the early seventeenth century. This was originally the screens passage, which defined the separation between the service areas to the left, and the symbolic heart of the household, the Great Hall, to the right. The fact that entry was through the screens passage reflects the survival of the medieval arrangement of houses into the early seventeenth century; by contrast, the exterior facade reflected a new sense of classical order, with two porches arranged symmetrically on either side of the bay window of the Great Hall.

In the nineteenth century the Entrance Hall was brought increasingly into the 'family' side of the house with the introduction of furniture and paintings, although a reminder of the traditional emphasis on the 'service' side was retained in the form of the set of leather fire buckets hanging from the oak beams. The furniture includes a marble-topped table moved here from the Great Hall sometime after 1836, a musical long-case clock, an oak armchair and cane-seated walnut chairs of the late seventeenth century. This eclectic combination of furnishings from many different periods is typical of the antiquarian taste of the third Lord Braybrooke.

2 GREAT HALL

The Great Hall dates from the building of the house (1603–14). In the Middle Ages households were run according to a complex system of hierarchy and deference, at the heart of which was the Great Hall, where communal meals took place. By the seventeenth century this system had largely disappeared and the hall form survived essentially as an anachronistic status symbol. The head of a household now generally preferred to withdraw to more private areas for eating and entertaining, although servants may have continued to take meals here.

The Great Hall rises through two storeys and is lit by five large windows on the west front, the centre window projecting in a large bow. The main architectural focus is the Jacobean oak screen at the north end, carved in high relief with grotesque masks and characteristic pairs of herms (male and female half-figures), raised on richly ornamented pedestals. The upper part of the screen forms the front of the gallery and is embellished with scrolling strapwork. The roof is largely original, although renewed and repaired. Each of the plaster panels is separated by oak beams and contains coloured armorial badges of the holders of the manor of Walden.

The interior of the Great Hall as it appears today was largely created by the third Lord Braybrooke in the 1820s. The screened Hall, with its display of heraldry, was a perfect expression of his antiquarian scholarship and nostalgia for the past. An occasion for medieval-style hospitality offered itself in 1852, when the Great Hall was used for a dinner celebrating the marriage of the third lord's eldest son; such a setting served to emphasise the antiquity of the family's lineage.

To recreate the Hall's original ambience, the third lord first had to undo the work of his eighteenth-century predecessors, removing white paint from the roof timbers and screen. The old and decayed wall panelling was replaced in 1829. The chimneypiece was enlarged and remodelled with old fragments, including the carved arms of Charles, seventh Earl of Suffolk and his wife, Arabella. Silk banners bearing the arms of owners of the manor of Walden from the twelfth to the nineteenth centuries were hung from the wall brackets on regimental lances. By contrast, modern innovations aimed at creating contemporary standards of comfort included the replacement of the old

ABOVE Detail of the north porch door. This was probably intended as the queen's entrance to the house; the carving depicts the rewards of Peace

BELOW Marble pedestal in the antique taste, purchased from Robert Adam in 1773 for the display of sculpture in the Great Hall

OPPOSITE The Great Hall as it was decorated and furnished by the third Lord Braybrooke in the 1820s. At the far end is the early seventeenth-century oak screen

casement windows with sash windows containing large glass plates in 1829.

The third lord used his inherited collections to create an idiosyncratic interior featuring objects esteemed for their age and historical associations. Two Coade stone figures, originally made for Sir John Griffin Griffin's neoclassical library, were painted to resemble oak and fitted into the chimneypiece, while the marble pedestal, purchased in 1773 from Robert Adam, was retained in the window bay. Reflecting the third lord's interest in British and medieval antiquities were a selection of oak carvings and furniture, notably the walnut chairs and the oak and inlaid court cupboard. The Flemish carving in the seventeenth-century-style case was purchased at an auction of Dutch furniture in 1826.

The Hall was further embellished with Indian shields, various fine firearms and a collection of swords. The helmets and epaulettes of two of the third lord's sons, who were killed during the Crimean War (1854–6), hang to the left of the chimneypiece.

The full-length portraits above the panelling are Cornwallis family pictures, while those on either side of the stone screen are mostly family members, monarchs and allies. The most notable portrait, hanging above the heating vent on the east wall, is of Margaret Audley, Duchess of Norfolk, by Hans Eworth; her son, the first Earl of Suffolk, was the builder of the great Jacobean house.

3 STAIRCASE

The stone screen at the south end of the Hall has historically been associated with the architect Sir John Vanbrugh, who carried out other work at Audley End in about 1708, although it may be the work of another architect, Nicholas Dubois. Dubois designed the staircase, which provides a ceremonial approach up to the Saloon, during the

mid-1720s. The Jacobean chapel was being demolished at this time and it seems that fragments were incorporated into the columns and entablature (lintel) framing the doorcase at the top of the stairs. The ceiling above the staircase is original, surviving from the Jacobean period. Nineteenth-century commentators considered these later features out of keeping with the rest of the Hall; Lord Braybrooke attributed it to the 'bad taste of Sir John Vanbrugh'.

4 SALOON

The Saloon is one of the most splendid of Audley End's interiors, the extravagance of the plaster ceiling befitting its Jacobean usage as the Great Chamber. Sir John Griffin Griffin retained this ceiling, with its thirty-two compartments, set between large pendants and outlined with patterned strapwork. According to Lord Braybrooke it was 'originally called the Fish Room, after the dolphins and sea-monsters represented in bold relief'. The frieze of Gothic quatrefoils probably dates from 1765–73, when Sir John first fitted out the Saloon. New panelling was installed with an elaborate frieze, and carved details were added from the demolished Long Gallery. The recesses within the round-headed arches were fitted with a series of ancestral portraits illustrating Sir John's descent from Sir Thomas Audley, the original recipient of Walden Abbey. The portraits of Sir John and his mother, and the early portraits of his Howard and Audley ancestors, were painted by the Italian artist Biagio Rebecca.

In 1784 Sir John was elevated to the peerage as Lord Howard de Walden, and over the following two years further decorative work was carried out to make the interior more splendid. As an acknowledgement of the family's ancient debt to the monarchy, Biagio Rebecca provided two more portraits – one of Henry VIII, who granted the abbey and its lands to Thomas Audley, and another of Elizabeth I, who created the barony of Howard de Walden. Rebecca also decorated the arms of the first Earl of Suffolk and his wife over the chimneypiece. At the same time the Saloon was painted white and enriched with gilding in the fashionable taste of the decade.

In place of Sir John's coordinated grandeur, Lord and Lady Braybrooke created an interior of their own time in the 1820s, transforming the

ABOVE *Dedication dated 1786, expressing Sir John's gratitude to those to whom he owed his position and ownership of Audley End*

TOP LEFT *Table top inlaid with pewter, brass and red tortoiseshell. Known as Boulle-work, this is a fine and early example of its type, mounted on an English oak base of the 1820s*

CENTRE *This mahogany sofa, made in about 1740, was reupholstered and painted in white and gilt to match the room. It was part of a suite of two sofas, eleven chairs and one stool*

OPPOSITE *The Saloon, with its seventeenth-century plaster ceiling, eighteenth-century family portraits and nineteenth-century carpet and furnishings*

ABOVE *The white ground carpet was made by Thomas Whitty of Axminster and was originally in the Saloon*

BELOW *A bust of the first Marquess Cornwallis by John Bacon RA. Above hangs a portrait of his grand-daughter, wife of the third Lord Braybrooke*

OPPOSITE *The Drawing Room, as furnished by the third Lord Braybrooke for his private use*

Saloon into a comfortable and informal living room. Visiting Audley End in 1847 Mrs Bancroft, wife of the American minister to England, described the Saloon thus: 'Not withstanding its vast size, the sofas and tables were so disposed all over the apartment as to give it the most friendly, warm and social aspect.'

The majority of Sir John's furniture remained in situ, placed against the walls in formal eighteenth-century style. By the 1850s, however, it was covered with loose covers of chintz, in colours chosen to complement the room's decorative scheme. Many contemporary pieces, such as the comfortable sofas, were simply loose-covered over the upholsterer's outer linen layer. This helped to create the informal air considered desirable in the early nineteenth century while also preserving furniture with fitted upholstery. The chairs flanking the chimneypiece were reupholstered in the nineteenth century; the needlework covers with a red quatrefoil ground surrounding conventional floral panels were probably made by the ladies of the family.

Furniture and soft furnishings introduced in the 1820s include the remarkable Axminster carpet, the circular Regency-period centre tables, around which groups of chairs could be informally placed, the rectangular rosewood sofa table (a new type), and some examples of fashionable French furniture. The pair of vitrines, or display cases, at the south end of the room are in the French style – although English-made – and contain family mementoes. Other furnishings were added to the Saloon as the century progressed, including the ottoman, a rare survival probably dating from the 1860s or 1870s.

The arrangement of plants on a table in the bay is illustrated in a watercolour of about 1850; plants were cultivated in greenhouses for interior display from the late eighteenth century. The curtains are reproductions of the light-damaged originals, which were of hand-woven damask and featured an eighteenth-century French pattern redrawn by a Spitalfields weaver. The colour red was Lord and Lady Braybrooke's first choice for their new reception rooms since it was particularly associated with ancient and noble interiors.

5 DRAWING ROOM

Lord Braybrooke created this room from two rooms belonging to the eighteenth-century State Bedroom suite. Paradoxically he fashioned an interior that was redolent of the seventeenth century, retained the white and gold decoration of the late eighteenth century, but was entirely of the 1820s in its function and furnishing. The ceiling was copied from the remains of the Jacobean

RIGHT *The South Library painted in about 1850. Its appearance has not altered since the early nineteenth century and, of all the rooms, it best expresses the continuity from one generation to another*

BELOW *Portrait of Jane Cornwallis, Lady Braybrooke, by Henry Pickersgill, 1834. Her husband hung it in his private Drawing Room*

CENTRE *Nineteenth-century visitors would have considered this walnut armchair, once the property of the poet Alexander Pope, one of the most evocative items at Audley End*

example in the adjoining South Library, while the frieze imitates details from the exterior porches. The Jacobean chimneypiece is possibly from the north wing of the house, brought here by Lord Braybrooke and fitted with an eighteenth-century steel grate from the State Dressing Room.

Lord Braybrooke used this room as his personal sitting room and hung it with the cream of Sir John's 'cabinet' pictures: Dutch, Italian and Flemish paintings of the type favoured by English gentlemen in the late eighteenth and early nineteenth centuries. The walls were hung with red flock wallpaper of an eighteenth-century design (since replaced), the traditional background for pictures. The third lord took obvious pride in this collection, formed entirely by Sir John. Particularly fine are *On the Shore at Egmond aan Zee* (1642) and *View of the Valkhof at Nijmegen* (1646), which hang to the right and left of the chimneypiece. They are by Jan van Goyen, the seventeenth-century Dutch master of landscape. The *View of the Campanile and the Doge's Palace* by Canaletto was at Audley End by 1797, and two other Venetian views attributed to Canaletto's studio were acquired by the second Lord Braybrooke. The portrait of Jane Cornwallis, Lady Braybrooke, by H W Pickersgill was the only modern addition to the collection in this room.

The room was furnished with inherited pieces, such as the five chairs brought from the Saloon. The two firescreens, in the Chinese taste, were decorated by Louisa Cornwallis, Lady Braybrooke's mother, in a European technique imitating oriental lacquer known as 'japanning'. The modern English Boulle-style cabinets for the display of porcelain represent more orthodox tastes, as do the fine 'antique' examples of French furniture: the Louis XV-period clock on a bracket

and the two French writing tables. One is signed by the cabinet-maker Montigny and is in the neoclassical style of the Louis XVI period, while the other is of an earlier date and in the rococo style, with floral marquetry, curved cabriole legs and scrolled ormolu (gilt bronze) mounts.

6 SOUTH LIBRARY

When the new Library was created in the 1820s, this room was turned into a private library and working area for Lord Braybrooke, where he gathered together his most prized relics. It contains the remnants of an original Jacobean ceiling, a mid-eighteenth-century frieze and a neoclassical chimneypiece by Robert Adam, installed in the 1780s.

The white and gold bookcases have adjustable shelves to accommodate outsize volumes, particularly topographical works. The collection is typical of the period, while also reflecting the particular interests of the third and fourth lords. There are books on gardening and agriculture, a selection of family bibles, and eighteenth- and nineteenth-century travel books on Europe, Australia, New Zealand and the Pacific. As might be expected, there are a number of books on heraldry and genealogy as well as military history, and a good collection of monographs on other country houses and their collections. Books purchased by Sir John are distinguished by their red leather covering and a gold chequer pattern on the spine.

The four chairs installed here by Lord Braybrooke were originally part of Sir John's suite of furniture for the Saloon. A 1786 invoice describes their yellow-and-white ground upholstery as 'patent tapestry', supplied by Thomas Moore of Moorfields. The backs of all the chairs and the two sofas were mounted with Howard lion crests and coronets. The unusual table screen, with a gilt frame and silk embroidered panel, was originally made for the Lady's State Dressing Room. These eighteenth-century items contrast strongly with others in the room, but it is apparent that each item has been selected for its historical associations.

An item of particular interest to the third Lord Braybrooke and his contemporaries would have been the walnut armchair with a triangular seat. A brass plaque on the back seat rail records: 'This chair once the property of Alexander Pope, was given as a keepsake to the nurse who attended him in his last illness. From her descendants it was obtained by Reverend Thomas Ashley, when Curate of the Parish of Binfield, and kindly presented by him to Lord Braybrooke in 1844.'

The library table is typical of early nineteenth-century furniture in seventeenth-century style. The 'metamorphic' armchair, with its distinctive Regency sabre legs, folds open to form library steps. The silk curtains are modern reproductions of one of Lord Braybrooke's most precious family relics. The originals were made of a crimson silk damask woven with the Neville saltire (a heraldic device similar to the St Andrew's cross), which had been presented in 1670 to his ancestor, Henry Nevill of Warfield, by Cosmo de Medici, the Grand Duke of Tuscany. Unlike other curtains in the house made during the nineteenth century, they were lined with silk as opposed to wool tammy, a mark of their importance.

The portraits of Sir John Griffin Griffin and his two wives, painted by Sir Benjamin West in 1772, were originally hung in Sir John's Library on the ground floor. Sir John is wearing the star of the Order of the Bath which he received in 1761.

7 LIBRARY

The Library was a new interior created by the third Lord Braybrooke in an historical manner achieved through the careful copying of existing details in the house. The plaster ceiling was copied from a Jacobean ceiling in the Dining Room while the frieze imitates that of the South Library. The arrangement of bays flanked by pilasters reproduces that of Sir John's Saloon, with the addition of fixed shelving for books. The frieze with strapwork and grotesque masks, and the white and gold decoration, executed in 1829, also emulate the Saloon scheme. The chimneypiece was moved here from the Howard Bedroom in the north wing.

Throughout the eighteenth century libraries tended to be masculine preserves and somewhat austere in their furnishing. By the 1820s, however, it had become fashionable for all the family to use

ABOVE *The Library. The arms of the Audley and Neville families on the chimneypiece link the third lord's family with the early owners of the house*

ABOVE *George II by Robert Edge Pine. Lord Howard purchased the portrait from the artist in 1784, nearly twenty-five years after it was painted. It now hangs in the Dining Room*

OPPOSITE *The Dining Room. The table is set as it would have been for the dessert course in the 1870s and 1880s, using a mid-nineteenth-century dessert service*

the library as an informal sitting room, and the furnishings reflected this dual use. A comfortable environment was created by loose-covered sofas, which were intended to be placed at right-angles to the fire, and armchairs and other contemporary furniture types, such as the table for reading and writing in front of the sofa. The circular centre table, of fashionable amboyna wood, provided a focus for informal gatherings, while the walnut portfolio stand could be opened up to examine large and precious volumes. The ebonised table with a green baize top was made for Lord Braybrooke, originally to contain the 'Scrapbook', a volume of accumulated prints, drawings and plans relating to the house. The American visitor Mrs Bancroft describes how social activities of a more relaxed nature took place in the Library. After breakfast and a tour of the house, 'We returned to the Library, a room as splendid as the Saloon, only instead of pictured panels it was surrounded by books in beautiful gilt bindings. In the immense bay window was a large Louis Quatorze table, round which the ladies all placed themselves at their embroidery, though I preferred looking over curious illuminated missals....' The Library accommodates many works of classical literature as well as volumes of standard eighteenth-century French and Italian literature, topographical and historical works on the English counties, archaeology and illustrated manuscripts.

The large bay window provided a good view over the parterre garden which was laid out in 1832. Although the morning light would have been favourable for needlework, reading or writing, it was also potentially damaging to the fragile fabric of the books. Several measures were taken to solve this problem, including inserting sash shutters into the window sill and fitting red striped blinds to the windows. The crimson damask curtains, trimmed with silk gimp (a looped braid) and held back with silk and wool tie-backs, are reproductions of originals which were in place by 1836.

The 'Brussels' carpet (as loop-piles were called from the time they were first made in the eighteenth century) is a reproduction also, seamed and laid in exactly the same way as the worn and faded original. It has vivid contemporary colours but draws on the Gothic motif of interlaced quatrefoils for its design.

8 DINING ROOM

The Dining Room was originally two Jacobean rooms, the plaster ceilings and friezes of which were retained when the dividing wall was removed. A Jacobean chimneypiece was copied to provide unity between the two rooms. As was customary in dining rooms, Lord Braybrooke hung the walls with family

portraits: a combination of Nevilles (brought from the family seat, Billingbear), Cornwallises and Howards. Apart from a single loss in this room, this remarkable collection, formed by inheritance and marriage, has been kept together to this day.

Above the sideboard at the far end of the room is a portrait of Lady Braybrooke's grandfather, the first Marquess Cornwallis, in his Garter robes. To its left is a portrait of her mother Louisa, Marchioness Cornwallis, by Sir Thomas Lawrence.

The richness of the interior fittings is augmented by the large hand-knotted Axminster carpet and wool velvet plush curtains with a pelmet trimmed with bullion fringe. The silk and wool tie-backs, which are modern reproductions, indicate the original colourings of this curtain scheme.

By contrast, the furniture was more functional and contemporary. One of the mahogany sideboards and the sectioned dining table are in the style of about 1810 and probably date from the second Lord Braybrooke's time. The second sideboard was probably made later for reasons of symmetry. The table could be sized according to the number of diners and the unused sections on their individual pedestals could then be used as side-tables. The simple mahogany chairs were originally covered with green leather, a material traditionally used in dining rooms as it was hard-wearing and did not retain the smell of food.

The Audley End accounts include details of 'Persons Dining' in the years 1867–75, in the time of Charles, fifth Lord Braybrooke. The figures for July 1872 show that on 14 July only three visitors dined, but that on 16 July ninety-five visitors were entertained. The average monthly figure was 700–900, of which the bulk was made up of servants. The accompanying remarks give some indication of the variety of visitors, such as 'Music Master', 'Miss Mildmay & Maid' and '14 for Dinner & one Gentleman for Lunch'.

9 SOUTH LOBBY

This area was a passage for guests and family moving from the Saloon to the Dining Room. It would also have formed the point of entry for the food, a highly unsatisfactory arrangement according to accepted nineteenth-century protocol, which dictated that service activities should be kept out of sight.

The oak staircase is the finer of two surviving staircases from the Jacobean house. It was embellished with further decoration by the third lord. The stairs lead up to bedrooms, probably for guests, and up another small staircase to a set of servants' rooms at the front of the house.

The landing area is hung with a set of five

seventeenth-century portraits of Ralph Grey, second Lord Grey of Werke, his wife, two sons and daughter Catherine, who married Richard Neville of Billingbear. The portraits accompanied Catherine to Billingbear, and the third lord brought them to Audley End. They are by the court artist Sir Peter Lely and have matching contemporary frames, exquisitely carved with undercutting and scrolling on the corners. The miniatures are largely Griffin portraits and formed part of the Countess of Portsmouth's inheritance. The finest example is by Nicholas Hilliard of Sir Thomas Griffin of Dingley, dated 1599.

10 PICTURE GALLERY

This gallery was formed by Sir John Griffin Griffin after 1763 to connect the north and south wings at first-floor level. The plaster ceiling was created in Jacobean style with interlacing strapwork. Sir John furnished it with country-style armchairs and hung it with a motley display of prints, watercolours and maps.

The third Lord Braybrooke chose to develop the room's potential as a picture gallery by introducing a series of important sixteenth-, seventeenth- and eighteenth-century Cornwallis portraits originating from Lady Braybrooke's ancestral homes, Brome Hall and Culford in Suffolk. The earliest portraits date from the sixteenth century, notably a portrait attributed to George Gower of Sir Thomas Cornwallis, the builder of Brome Hall, in 1558. Other fine portraits include that of Charles, second Lord Cornwallis by John Michael Wright dating from the 1660s, and the Hon Henrietta Maria Cornwallis by Sir Peter Lely. At the far end of the Picture Gallery, above the display cabinet, is a painting of Billingbear, the Neville family seat in Berkshire.

Throughout the nineteenth century the Picture Gallery served as another comfortable and informal family sitting room, connecting the family bedrooms with the reception rooms. The fourth lord's natural history collection gradually accumulated here, initially displayed in cases of various sizes piled up in an arbitrary fashion, but mounted in fitted oak cases soon after the fourth lord's succession in 1858. (See page 54 for a discussion of the natural history collection). By 1891 a miscellaneous collection of ceramics embellished the tops of the cases, including oriental ceramics, ancient Delft ware and Sir John's blue and white Worcester jugs and washbowls, originally used in the State Apartment.

The red wool plush curtains and pelmets trimmed with bullion fringe date from the early twentieth century; at the same time the floor was relaid with a Brussels carpet in two shades of red and black, with a seaweed-pattern ground and entwined floral border.

11 NORTH LOBBY

From this level the staircase leads up to family bedrooms and to the nineteenth-century nurseries used by the third Lord Braybrooke's children.

The case to the left of the door from the Picture Gallery contains a pair of Great Bustards, once common on Salisbury Plain but now long extinct. Two family portraits, in pierced rococo-style frames, hang above this case and that on the other side. The gilt cast of the Corbridge Lanx, hanging to the left of the marble-topped heating vent, illustrates the fourth lord's interest in archaeology. This celebrated late Roman dish was discovered at Corbridge in Northumberland in 1735.

12 CHAPEL VESTIBULE

In the Jacobean period this area was the music gallery overlooking the Great Hall. Subsequently it served as the family entrance to the Chapel. The pictures have religious themes and represent

NATIONAL MONUMENTS RECORD

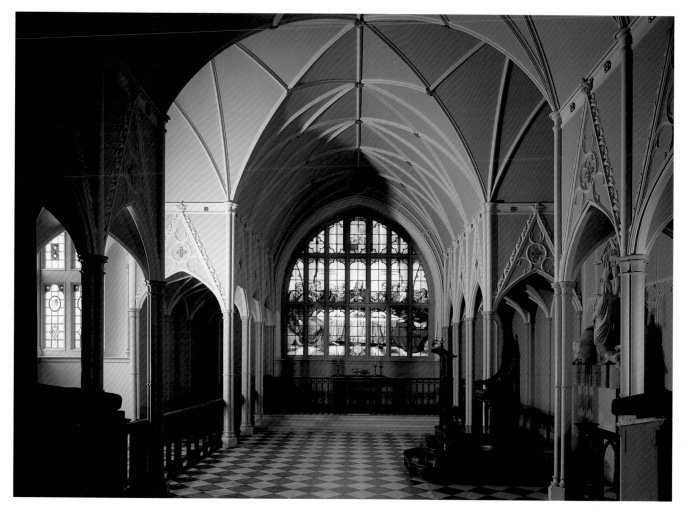

conventional nineteenth-century piety. Mrs Bancroft relates how in 1847 the guests would assemble in the Picture Gallery at half-past nine before entering the Chapel for morning prayers.

13 CHAPEL

Sir John Griffin Griffin's Chapel is a rare surviving example of a chapel in the late eighteenth-century Gothick style, with all its furniture intact. By the 1820s private chapels were becoming less common and, if the third lord had pursued his initial intention of converting the Chapel into a dining room, it may not have been replaced elsewhere. The third lord disliked its profusely ornamented fan vaulting, arcading and columns made of timber, lath and plaster painted to imitate stone. He objected to this essentially decorative interpretation of the Gothic style, which he considered archaeo-logically dishonest.

In the late 1760s Sir John commissioned the master builder John Hobcroft to produce the designs and carry out the work for his new chapel,

including all the furnishings. The floor was covered with an oilcloth painted to simulate a Portland and Bremen stone pavement; the current covering is a reproduction. The Chapel was further embellished in 1786 with heraldic decoration linking the Audley, Griffin and Howard families.

Morning prayers were said in the Chapel every day except on Sundays when the family joined the local community in Saffron Walden Church. The family pew was comfortably furnished with a set of painted chairs inset with the Howard crest. Although re-covered in recent years, the hassocks are also original. Other comforts were provided by a Wilton carpet, a fire burning in the chimneypiece and an adjacent water-closet. The indoor servants sat in the organ gallery while the outdoor servants and kitchen staff, who entered via a staircase from the service areas below, used the plain oak benches and brown leather kneelers. These functional items, together with the communion table, were made by the estate joiners.

The carved chair and lectern are made of olive wood and were carved by the accomplished

ABOVE *The interior of the Chapel. The stained and painted glass window of 'Our Saviour's Last Supper' was made by William Peckitt of York in 1771*

furniture-maker and carver Sefferin Alkin. The plaster half-size model of the first Marquess Cornwallis was made by Charles Rossi from the Marquess's tomb monument in St Paul's Cathedral. It was given to the third lord in 1835 by the Marquess's daughter, Lady Mary Singleton.

14 LADY BRAYBROOKE'S SITTING ROOM

This and the following rooms form a private apartment used in the nineteenth century by the third Lord Braybrooke and his wife. The wallpaper is a modern reproduction of a design used throughout the apartment dating from about 1830.

The third Lady Braybrooke used this as a dressing room and morning room. It was an informal environment in which she could conduct everyday activities such as letter-writing. Comfortable armchairs were covered with chintz loose covers to match the wallpaper and curtains. Other furniture included the French corner cupboards of the Louis XV period, the slightly later kingwood and marquetry armoire of about 1770 and the marble-top commode or chest of drawers, of similar date. These items may have been part of Lady Braybrooke's inheritance or new purchases in keeping with contemporary English taste. The late sixteenth-century French oak cupboard was bought by Lord and Lady Braybrooke during their visit to Antwerp in 1829 and the green tortoiseshell bracket clock belonged to Sir John. The fine portrait to the left of the armoire is of the Countess of Portsmouth, painted in 1762 by Thomas Hudson. Alongside it are portraits of Lord Braybrooke's Neville grandfather by Zoffany, and of Lady Braybrooke's father, the second Marquess Cornwallis, by Hoppner. Opposite is a portrait of the third lord at the age of twenty-one. Over the years Lady Braybrooke added a group of oval portraits of her children, and prints of relations and friends.

By 1891 Florence, wife of the fifth lord, had added further layers of rich furnishings in keeping with late nineteenth-century taste. The fashion for furniture in the style of the late eighteenth century meant that she could simply bring Sir John's furniture out of storage and have it french-polished and reupholstered. The density of the furnishings is typical of the last quarter of the nineteenth century, the effect increased by table-

covers and antimacassars in exotic fabrics and a collection of antique ceramics. In the twentieth century this became the family sitting room.

15 NEVILLE BEDROOM

Originally the dressing room of the Jacobean State Apartment, this room is one of the few spaces in the house to remain in its original form, with its Jacobean frieze intact on all four walls. In about 1700 the walls were panelled with curved relief (bolection) moulding, part of which survives. The third Lord Braybrooke probably inserted the Jacobean oak chimneypiece, which evidently originated in a smaller room.

This room and the dressing room beyond now hold displaced furnishings from the Red Bedroom suite on the ground floor, the second-best guest bedroom suite in the nineteenth century. The bed had originally been supplied to Sir John Griffin Griffin in 1766 by the London upholsterer Paul Saunders. The original mixed silk and wool damask still survives on the inside of the tester (canopy) with its shaped cresting. The lacquer furniture and the gilt mirror have always been in the same room as the bed; the night tables are of comparable date, about 1760.

16 NEVILLE DRESSING ROOM

The elaborate low-relief ceiling dates from Sir John's time, when this room served as his wife's dressing room. The door in the outer east wall, like that in the next room, leads through to water closets, further dressing rooms and a staircase to the ground floor.

A number of the portraits are of friends and colleagues of Sir John. The four Worcester vases on the chimneypiece were painted by the third Lord Braybrooke's mother-in-law, Louisa, Marchioness Cornwallis.

LEFT *Dutch walnut cupboard in the Neville Dressing Room. It has fine ivory and ebony inlay and was one of the third lord's foreign purchases*

CENTRE *Worcester porcelain vases with painted decoration by Louisa Cornwallis, Lady Braybrooke's mother*

OPPOSITE *Lady Braybrooke's Sitting Room with its French eighteenth-century furniture. The English furniture was added by her successor, Florence, wife of the fifth lord*

ABOVE *Conventional neoclassical motif embroidered on the inside of the tester (canopy) of the State Bed*

RIGHT *The Howard Sitting Room photographed in the early twentieth century. It is furnished in typical 'country-house' style*

OPPOSITE *The Howard Bedroom. The India blue taffety of the bed-hangings was decorated with embroidery in coloured silk and metallic threads by J Seneschal*

BELOW *Detail of embroidery on the upper valance of the bed*

17 HOWARD DRESSING ROOM

From the third Lord Braybrooke's time on, this and the following rooms formed another suite of rooms comprising a dressing room, bedroom and sitting room. These were guest rooms, and were never as densely furnished with the bric-à-brac of everyday life as the equivalent family rooms. The entire suite was originally carpeted with a fitted Brussels carpet.

Sir John built this room to use as his dressing room in 1784, and it continued to fulfil that function as part of the guest suite in the nineteenth century. Like the Howard Bedroom beyond, it now contains an ensemble of furniture displaced from the nineteenth-century State Bedroom suite on the ground floor. The daybed and the washstand were both acquired in advance of a visit to Audley End by the Duke of Gloucester and his wife in 1819.

The paintings include a view of Windsor Castle and portraits of the young Countess of Portsmouth, Anne Rainsford and Anne Heydon, ancestors of Sir John Griffin Griffin.

18 HOWARD BEDROOM

In the seventeenth century this was part of the Queen's State Apartment; the surviving Jacobean ceiling is only about a third of its original size. During the nineteenth and early twentieth centuries it served as the bedroom of the guest suite and was furnished with a four-post bedstead with chintz hangings.

It now contains the State Bed, although the bed is, in fact, much too important for the room and has no historical connections with it. The bed, together with the stool, armchairs and the portrait of Queen Charlotte, were all commissioned by Sir John Griffin Griffin for his State Bedroom (now the South Library) in anticipation of a royal visit following his elevation to the peerage in 1784. In the third Lord Braybrooke's time the bed and accompanying furniture were moved to the new suite of guest rooms on the ground floor, where

COUNTRY LIFE

they were used by Mrs Bancroft and her husband during their visit in 1847. Other furnishings and pictures were gradually added to the ensemble, including the gilded gesso table of about 1730.

The State Bed is one of the most important surviving late eighteenth-century beds and was made by the London firm of Chipchase and Lambert in 1786. The curved cornice carries a baron's coronet and military trophies in the corner and the Howard crest in the centre. The lions' masks on the bed unified it with the chimneypiece from the original State Bedroom (transferred here in the 1820s). The bed-hangings were described by Emilia Clayton, Sir John's sister-in-law, as being 'made up with the greatest taste I ever saw'.

19 HOWARD SITTING ROOM

Since most of its original contents are no longer at Audley End the Sitting Room has been recreated, using the evidence of surviving records, in the country-house style of the late nineteenth and early twentieth centuries. The fine mahogany knee-hole 'partner's desk' – with drawers on both sides – is of mid-eighteenth-century date and may originally have come from Sir John's Library. The large oriental black lacquer chest and the smaller seventeenth-century chest on a modern stand may also have belonged to Sir John: like other furniture of his period they became fashionable again in the last decades of the nineteenth century. The small ebonised bookcase with a rosewood veneered top is of the 1820s.

The pictures were probably chosen for this room by the third lord; they are all recorded as hanging here in 1871. They mostly relate to the

ABOVE *The Butler's Pantry, with its original cupboards. The wall colour was traditionally used for service areas because of the cheapness of the pigments*

plate rack and swill tub. The kitchen contained a long table in the middle, dressers at each end, chopping blocks, a salt box, smaller deal tables and wood-bottom chairs. The range and oven featured spits and skewers. The kitchen maids' and cook's rooms were over the kitchen.

By 1797 the servants' hall, adjacent to the new kitchen, was furnished with two long deal tables and forms. Beyond was the laundry with a range and iron stove. Further equipment included a mangle, ironing table, wash tubs, drying frame and clothes horse. Most of the servants' accommodation was in the stables but the footman and other senior indoor servants appear to have had bedrooms on the upper levels of the house.

The service areas have been restored as far as possible, but much of the original equipment has gone and the rooms have been converted for other purposes.

Neville family, including a 'conversation piece' depicting the second Lord Braybrooke, together with friends and a guide, examining the classical ruins of Rome. The portraits of the Duke of Brunswick and Prince Ferdinand were copied for Sir John, who had served under both princes during the Seven Years' War (1756–63).

20 NORTH STAIRS

Although the stairs are not in their original position and the flights have been narrowed, this is the second staircase to have survived from the Jacobean house. It is plainer than that on the south side, indicating that the rooms it served were less important.

THE SERVICE AREAS

The life enjoyed by the occupants of Audley End over four centuries would not have been possible without the efficient organisation of the service areas. They have remained mostly to the north of the screens passage, as originally devised in the early seventeenth century, although some of their functions have changed as patterns of service have altered. In 1763 a new block, designed by Robert Adam, was built within a walled enclosure adjacent to the house; it housed the brewhouse, dairy and bakery. A new kitchen was also added, linked to the house by a narrow corridor.

As the role of female servants, particularly that of the housekeeper, became more important in the eighteenth century, a housekeeper's room was set up beyond the valet's room alongside the Entrance Hall. There was also a pantry for the storage of food; larders complete with pickling tubs, meat hook and bread bin; and a scullery with a copper

21 BUTLER'S PANTRY

The butler was responsible for the upkeep of the family plate, decanters and glasses and for overseeing the service of food and wine. He was even required to ensure surveillance of the silver overnight: in 1797 this room contained a folding bed, with bars at the windows for extra security. In the nineteenth century he was given a separate bedroom in the adjacent room. Plate in day-to-day use would have been locked away in the cupboards, which were lined with baize to protect it from knocks. The furnishings include a pine work table and trays and a large lead-lined sink for the cleaning of plate. The locking chests were used for storing or moving the plate between houses.

On display in the cupboards is a portion of the family plate. In general it is arranged in groups according to its original ownership, as indicated by the crests that were usually added when pieces were commissioned or purchased. This gives a coherent picture of the chronology of the collection and of dining etiquette at different periods. (See page 52 for a more detailed discussion of the silver collection.)

The first double case contains pieces from the Rainsford family. Anne Rainsford had married James, second Lord Griffin in 1684, and the pieces were part of Sir John's inheritance which subsequently passed into the Neville family. The second case contains the plate given to Elizabeth Griffin during her marriage to Henry Grey, and the third holds items from her second marriage to the Earl of Portsmouth. The fourth and fifth cases display the magnificent plate of Sir John Griffin Griffin, while the sixth contains Neville family silver. The seventh case is densely arranged with similar types of items grouped together, as it might have been put away by the butler, and the eighth contains items bearing the Cornwallis crest, indicating that they were part of Lady Braybrooke's inheritance. The final case contains miscellaneous late nineteenth- and twentieth-century items.

MUSEUM ROOM
(not accessible to the public)

A dressing room in Sir John's time, this was appropriated by the fourth Lord Braybrooke as a private museum to house his considerable collections of objects relating to classical antiquity, geology and natural history. A watercolour of about 1845 (below) shows Samian ware lined up on shelves, the remains of a Roman pavement mounted on a plinth, and geological specimens neatly arranged in a display case. The air of scientific enquiry is belied by a highly domestic decorative scheme, complete with wallpaper, curtains and carpet, making the overall impression one of pleasing idiosyncrasy. The room was preserved by the family until the 1950s when the collection was sold to a museum and the interior dismantled for administrative use. It is hoped, however, that in future some elements of the fourth lord's arrangement will be reinstated.

Like his father, the fourth lord was essentially an antiquarian, although his academic pursuits focused on somewhat different subjects. These included not only ornithology but also archaeological work on prehistoric British sites, and he was involved in many excavations carried out in Essex and the surrounding locality.

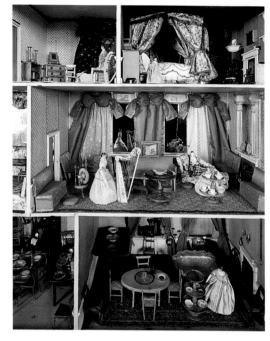

LEFT *Interior of the Dolls' House. The curtains and bed-hangings were probably made by the third lord's children from scraps of fabric. They carefully imitate the fashionable taste of about 1830*

BELOW *Watercolour of about 1845 of the Museum Room, with its eclectic collections of antiquities, ethnography and natural history*

22 SMALL DINING ROOM

Used as a steward's room in the eighteenth century, by the late 1920s this had become an informal dining room for the young family of the seventh Lord Braybrooke. It was smaller, warmer and less formal than the first-floor Dining Room, and was also closer to the kitchen. It currently houses the Dolls' House that belonged to the third lord's children.

23 LOWER GALLERY

In the eighteenth century an open arcade was erected by Sir John Griffin Griffin beneath the Picture Gallery on the first floor, linking the north and south wings at this level. In 1863 it was enclosed and glazed and the overspill of the fourth lord's natural history cases from the Picture Gallery was housed here.

24 SOUTH STAIRS

This is the richer of the two surviving staircases from the Jacobean period. The third lord stripped it of its eighteenth-century white paint and embellished the newel posts with heraldic beasts. On the stairs hangs one of his most prized possessions: a framed engraving of the Jacobean Audley End. It is one of a series of survey pictures showing the house in its original form, undertaken by Henry Winstanley of Littlebury in about 1676, when Audley End was a royal palace.

The very large painting with the lavish frame is of Billingbear and its environs by Jan Griffier the Younger. This was the ancestral seat of the Nevilles in Berkshire; Windsor Castle can be glimpsed in the background. The house was demolished in 1926.

25 SOUTH CORRIDOR (RED BEDROOM SUITE)

In the eighteenth century the rooms on the north side of this wing were part of the suite of rooms created for Sir John Griffin Griffin by Robert Adam in the 1770s. The corridor was cut through in the

1820s, destroying Sir John's parlours where he had hung his fine collection of Old Master paintings. On the left new servants' rooms were created. At the east end of the wing the former Library was dismantled and replaced by the Red Bedroom suite, containing the Red Bed (now seen in the Neville Bedroom). Adam's grand reception rooms on the south side were converted into a State Bedroom suite, but have since been restored to their late eighteenth-century appearance.

26 18TH-CENTURY TOPOGRAPHICAL PAINTINGS

At the end of the corridor, in the nineteenth-century dressing room, is a collection of views of the house and park, most of which were painted by William Tomkins in the 1780s. The Nevilles took these pictures to Billingbear in the nineteenth century but they returned to Audley End in 1916.

THE ROBERT ADAM ROOMS

In contrast to the work Sir John Griffin Griffin carried out in the Saloon, the Picture Gallery and elsewhere, which demonstrates his desire to retain and emphasise the antiquity of the house, his remodelling of the ground floor of the south wing was intended to create a suite of rooms in the height of neoclassical taste. They were designed by Robert Adam in the mid-1760s and were largely completed and furnished by 1771.

The new suite comprised eight rooms, those on the south forming the 'Great Apartment' while the two on the north provided more intimate accommodation. The design and fitting out of the rooms is recorded in great detail in archives, and their final appearance and function is given in the inventory taken on Sir John's death in 1797.

Unlike the other rooms in the house, which are shown as they have evolved through different generations, these rooms were reinstated to their eighteenth-century appearance some thirty years ago, leaving no evidence of the nineteenth-century remodelling. Where it survives they are furnished with their original furniture, supplemented by reproductions of the original textiles. The aim is to give an accurate impression of formal late eighteenth-century living, although the exact sequence of rooms cannot be experienced since the principal room, the Library, was demolished in the 1820s. To give a more complete picture of the original furnishings, the 1797 inventory entries for each room have been included in italics below.

27 LITTLE DRAWING ROOM

In all the rooms on the ground floor apart from the Library, Robert Adam was faced with the problem of relatively low ceilings. In the case of the Little Drawing Room this constraint was turned to advantage, resulting in a richly decorated, intimate room ideally suited to its role as a withdrawing room to which the ladies would retire, leaving the gentlemen to continue talking and drinking in the Dining Parlour.

An early unexecuted ceiling design by Robert Adam, inscribed 'Ceiling in the taste of the Paintings of the Ancients', makes clear his aim to create a thoroughly up-to-date neoclassical interior. The decorative painting on the walls, ceiling, doors and shutters is derived from ancient grotesque ornament seen by Adam in Italy, and was executed by Biagio Rebecca in 1773. Rebecca also painted the group of five grisaille panels (monochrome paintings simulating sculpture), which were based on published illustrations of ancient Roman examples.

It is clear from the relationship of the furniture to the architecture of the room, as well as from references in the bills, that Adam was involved in the furniture designs. The suite of furniture was supplied by the London company of Taitt and Gordon in 1771. It is of very high quality water-gilding, as opposed to the cheaper method of oil-gilding. All but one piece has survived (one of two small 'scrole seats'). A comparison of the costs reveals that the most expensive item was not the large scroll-headed couch at £30, but the mirror plate, at £73 10s.

The inventory taken on Sir John's death in 1797 reveals the care taken of such valuable pieces: the furniture had two sets of covers, outer ones of white flannel and inner ones of cotton, which served to protect the precious silk brocade upholstery. The same brocade was used for a wall hanging in the recess, and for festoon curtains which survive, though somewhat cut-down.

LEFT *Set of architectural drawings by Placido Columbani, c.1786, recording the completed decoration in the Little Drawing Room.* TOP *The door, shutter-cases and other details.* CENTRE *Plan and wall elevations.* BOTTOM *The elaborate painted ceiling*

*One large Couch, 2 small Do. 2 Bolsters,
2 Pillows, 4 Stools, cover'd with flower'd Sattin,
Cotton & flannel Covers, 2 festoon window curtains
to match, 4 Japan'd Chairs cane seats, a Carpet of
Moores Tapestry, a Piece of Baize for do. A Small
Octagon work table with a Glass top, Carv'd & Gilt
frame, Venetian Blinds, Sattin Hangings for recess,
paper covering to do. on canvas.*

28 GREAT DRAWING ROOM

In the eighteenth century this room would have
formed the approach to the even greater richness of
the Little Drawing Room. The lack of height is
more apparent despite Adam's attempts to
manipulate proportions by lowering the dado rail
and reducing the height of the furniture.

The most striking feature of the room is the use of a
three-colour silk tissue for the wall-hangings and
festoon curtains (the existing fabric is a modern copy).
Such rich fabrics enjoyed popularity in the late 1760s.
It was bought from a mercer at a cost of 18s 6d a yard,
almost three times the cost of the silk used in the Dining
Parlour. The fabric itself formed the decoration of
the room and was not concealed by paintings.

Almost the entire suite of furniture, comprising
fourteen pieces of seat furniture and two pier glasses
and tables, survives. It is arranged formally as it
would have been in the eighteenth century; as guests
arrived a footman would have brought forward a
chair for use. These pieces too were protected by
case covers of green-and-white striped linen, while
the marquetry table tops were equipped with
stamped leather covers which would only have been
removed for visitors of the highest status. Some years
after the room was fitted up, green Venetian blinds
were installed to the south-facing windows to
provide further protection to the furnishings.

The group of cane-seated chairs in the bay is a later
introduction. Dating from 1793, they show the trend
away from the grand gilded furniture of the 1760s and
1770s to more informal and easily moveable pieces.

*An Axminster Carpet, 8 Elbow
Chairs, 2 Sophas, 4 Window
stools, cover'd with Sattin &
Covers to do. a pair of inlaid Pier
tables, on carv'd & Gilt frames, a
pair of large french plate pier
Glasses in Square gilt frames, an
inlaid pembroke table, 2 fire
screens, 8 Japan'd chairs Cane
bottoms, a Plaister Groupe (Venus
& Cupid) by Flaxman, Venetian
Blinds, Sattin Hangings to Room
& paper covering to do. on canvas.*

29 VESTIBULE

Entered through the double doors from the
South Stairs, this room would have formed the
route by which eighteenth-century visitors
approached the Great Drawing Room or Dining
Parlour. When looking through the two Drawing
Rooms the extent of the original enfilade or vista
can be appreciated; it would also have taken in
the now-demolished Library.

The Vestibule was always intended as a
circulation room, and was originally sparsely
furnished with a pair of pedestals designed by
Adam to support candelabra. These were moved
to the State Bedroom suite in 1786 and replaced
by a table and set of six chairs.

30 DINING PARLOUR

Adam faced even greater difficulties in trying to
create a fashionable interior for the Dining Parlour,
for, in addition to the lowness of the room, the two
Jacobean bays are of different sizes and configu-
rations. To overcome this problem he omitted all
ceiling decoration, and created symmetrical inner
areas defined by the two screens of columns.

The size of the Jacobean windows meant that
shutters could not easily be fitted, so curtains were
provided although this was generally avoided in
dining rooms to prevent smells
from lingering in the fabric.

The curtains also served to
disguise the differences in the two
bays. Originally of lustring (a
glossy silk) matching the pea-
green paintwork, these were
replaced in 1786 by curtains of
green taberay (a silk and linen
fabric), replicas of which hang
here today. By this time fabric
blinds had also been fitted.

The room contains several

original items of furniture and is arranged as it would have been in the eighteenth century. In contrast to the nineteenth-century Dining Room upstairs, no central table was kept in the room. Instead a variety of tables for different numbers of people were kept in adjacent rooms and corridors and brought in for use. Thus when the room was not being used for dining it could be used as a 'parade room', where costly items such as the carpet could be shown off to their full advantage, and guests might admire the views from the windows.

The carpet is a copy of a rare eighteenth-century turkey-pattern Axminster. The bold pattern and colouring provide a contrast to the dominant colour of the walls and curtains, which are replicas of the 'rich green striped watered taberay' supplied in 1786. As in the Great Drawing Room there were no pictures, though when the Dining Parlour was in use the silver and gilt plate would have made an impressive display.

Twelve Mahy. Chairs, cov'd with leather, a Mahy Octagon dining Table, 2 marble slabs on Mahy. Frames, Four florence Vases on Pedestals, Derbyshire ornaments, & 2 vases, 4 fire screens, a Back do. and Axmr. Turkey Carpet, and Oilcloth, 2 festoon taberay window curtains & balance weights, Blinds, a Grate shovel, tongs, poker and fender, 2 Mahy. Stands for Wine tubs, a painted Chimney Stop by Rebecca.

31 LOBBY

On a floor plan of 1786 this room is referred to as 'Anti Room', but it must have had a dual function, as a storage area for tables, chairs and dumb-waiters, and as a serving area for food brought in procession across the Great Hall. The two pairs of double doors are part of the nineteenth-century remodelling. The original doors would have matched that on the east wall.

To leave the house, retrace your steps through the Great Hall and back into the Entrance Hall.

THE OWNERS
OF AUDLEY END

THE MEDIEVAL MONASTERY

FAR RIGHT *Thomas Howard, fourth Duke of Norfolk. Ironically, investigations into his alleged treason were launched while Queen Elizabeth was staying at Audley End in the summer of 1569*

The Benedictine priory of Walden was established in about 1140 by Prior William and a small group of monks. Its founder was Geoffrey de Manderville, Earl of Essex. In 1190 Richard I raised the priory to the status of an abbey, which, by the early sixteenth century, had become immensely powerful and wealthy. On 22 March 1538, however, the abbey was suppressed and its possessions surrendered to the Crown; five days later they were given to Sir Thomas Audley, Lord Chancellor of England.

ABOVE *Queen Elizabeth I, a copy of the 'Rainbow' portrait attributed to Marcus Gheeraerts the Younger. The queen created the barony of Howard de Walden in 1597 to reward Thomas Howard for his naval achievements*

RIGHT *Sir Thomas Audley who, after the dissolution of the monasteries, acquired the lands and abbey buildings which became the site of the future Audley End House*

SIR THOMAS AUDLEY

The career of Thomas Audley (1488–1544) was one of political achievement and intrigue. He held high office throughout much of the long and turbulent reign of Henry VIII. A lawyer by training, he was shrewd, of exceptional intelligence, unsubtle, ruthless and, by his own admission, lacking devotion to 'any sects of religion'. This latter was a useful quality in the man charged, as Speaker of Parliament, with overseeing England's break with the Roman Catholic Church.

Audley was of humble origins but he aspired to the highest rank. He was appointed Lord Chancellor in

1533 and in the same year conferred legal authority on Henry's divorce from Catherine of Aragon, enabling the king to marry Anne Boleyn. Two years later he again came to the king's assistance, passing the death sentence on Sir Thomas More, who had opposed Henry's religious reforms. In 1536 Audley presided over another dubious trial, ironically that of Anne Boleyn, who was convicted on fraudulent charges of treason and executed in the Tower.

Audley recognised that his reputation had suffered as a result of these notorious acts, writing to a correspondent that the 'eight hundred a year' afforded to him as Lord Chancellor was 'scarcely sufficient to pay my housekeeping, let alone compensate for my dishonour'. However, he was amply rewarded for his part in the dissolution of the monasteries: in addition to Walden Abbey he received the Priory of Christ Church, Aldgate, and St Botolph's Priory, Colchester.

In 1539 Audley's skills were called on once more when he brokered the annulment of Henry's calamitous six-month marriage to the Protestant Anne of Cleves. He also played a key role in the trial and execution of the young queen Catherine Howard.

In 1538 he married his second wife, Elizabeth, sister of the powerful Duke of Suffolk (who bore no relation to the Earls of Suffolk, later owners of Audley End). They had two daughters, only one of whom, Margaret, survived; it was she who inherited Audley End on the death of her mother in 1557.

THOMAS HOWARD, FOURTH DUKE OF NORFOLK

Margaret Audley was only four years old when her father died. At fourteen she married Lord Henry Dudley, but following his death she was married again, to Thomas Howard, fourth Duke of Norfolk (1536–72). This union established a Howard link with Audley End which would remain unbroken for almost two centuries. It produced five children, from whom are descended the Earls of Suffolk, Berkshire, Carlisle and Bristol. It was the Earl of Suffolk who would later be responsible for building the present house.

Norfolk was an ambitious courtier and a close confidant of Elizabeth I. However, he suffered a disastrous fall from favour after being implicated in a plot to place Mary Queen of Scots on the throne of England, culminating in his execution in 1572. Margaret had died in 1564 when she was only twenty-four; she is buried in the Norfolk family vaults at the parish church of Framlingham in Suffolk.

Following Norfolk's death his brother, the Earl of Northampton, took up residence at Audley End, undertaking the role of guardian to the duke's young children. It was probably Northampton who received Queen Elizabeth when she visited Audley End in 1578.

THOMAS HOWARD, FIRST EARL OF SUFFOLK

Thomas Howard (1561–1626) was the Duke of Norfolk's second son, and oldest son of his second marriage to Margaret Audley. He probably inherited Audley End in 1582. Thomas had an impressive naval career, and was knighted for his part in bringing about the failure of King Philip of Spain's invasion force, the Armada. As commander of the 38-gun *Golden Lion* he played a central role in the battles that saw the destruction of much of the Spanish fleet. His success continued in 1597 when he commanded one of four squadrons which took part in the taking of Cadiz (two of the others were commanded by

LEFT *Thomas Howard, first Earl of Suffolk, from the sequence of family portraits in the Saloon*

BELOW *Portrait of James I from the Audley End collection. James created Thomas Howard first Earl of Suffolk and bestowed on him the highest government appointment of Lord Treasurer*

Raleigh and Essex). In recognition of his achievements he was granted the barony of Howard de Walden in 1597.

Following Elizabeth I's death in 1603 Thomas was amongst the select company gathered at the royal palace Theobalds House in Hertfordshire to pledge allegiance to the new king, James I. Acceptance at court was critical to political advancement and Thomas evidently achieved this, for within two months he was created Earl of Suffolk and Lord Chamberlain of the Household. In his new role it was essential that Thomas possess a suitable residence by which to promote his personal power and to accommodate the king and his entourage when they visited. In the year of James's succession, therefore, the earl embarked on the construction of what was to be one of the largest houses in England on the site of Lord Audley's demolished mansion.

Work on the palatial new house was completed by 1614, the year in which Suffolk was elevated to the position of Lord Treasurer of England. He may have been helped in the design by his uncle, the Earl of Northampton, who had recently built 'a noble structure at Charing Crosse' (Northampton House). Audley End House cost over £200,000 to build and furnish, a vast sum for the time. The visiting James I remarked that it was too great a house for a king, but might suit a Lord Treasurer.

In 1615 the king visited the nearby university city of Cambridge where Suffolk, as Chancellor of the university, played the host. The festivities at are reputed to have cost £1000 a day. The earl's

passion for building – besides Audley End he built Charlton Park, Wiltshire and remodelled Lulworth Castle and Bindon House, Dorset – and extravagant lifestyle eventually caught up with him; in 1618, amidst whispers of corruption, he was relieved of the office of Lord Treasurer. In November of the following year he was found guilty of 'divers misdemeaners ... translating of debts ... extorcion, and bribery', and was committed to the Tower along with his countess, Catherine Knevet. Both were released some nine days later having agreed to pay a fine of £30,000, a sum that was later reduced to £7000. Nevertheless, the episode resulted in a loss of wealth and status from which subsequent Earls of Suffolk never fully recovered. The earl died in 1626 but his debts outlived him.

THE SECOND, THIRD AND FOURTH EARLS OF SUFFOLK

The first earl was succeeded by his eldest son, Theophilus (1584–1640). Despite ill health, the second earl struggled to maintain his status, managing in 1628 to secure the valuable appointment of Lord Warden of the Cinque Ports. The financial situation was still desperate, however, when his son James, the third Earl of Suffolk (1620–88), inherited Audley End in 1640. In the following year the family residence in London (Suffolk House, formerly Northampton House) was sold and a large quantity of plate pawned, raising about £50,000. Despite this, the

CHARLES II AT AUDLEY END

During the autumn of 1668 Charles's queen, Catherine of Braganza, held her court at Audley End. Here she was visited by the king, who spent his time 'divertising himself ... at Newmarket and visiting several forts and towns on the sea-coast'. After these early visits, however, the king lost interest in Audley End. Succeeding monarchs also paid it little attention although extensive work was undertaken, much of it under the direction of Sir Christopher Wren, Surveyor of the King's Works. The building's condition continued to deteriorate and in 1701 Wren urged King William III to divest himself of this unnecessary burden. Accordingly the property was returned to the Howards, though only after Henry, fifth Earl of Suffolk, had agreed to relinquish any claims to the £20,000 which was still outstanding from the original purchase price of £50,000.

DECLINE AND FALL: THE FIFTH TO THE TENTH EARLS OF SUFFOLK, 1691–1745

The first half of the eighteenth century – a period in which many people gained enormous wealth as a result of Britain's overseas trade and territorial expansion – was, ironically, one of declining fortunes for succeeding Earls of Suffolk. The fifth earl was seventy-five when Audley End was returned to him, and he died in 1709. His son Henry managed to secure a number of

deterioration of the estate continued to place great burdens on the family.

When civil war erupted in 1642 James, like many of his East Anglian neighbours, sided with Parliament. In 1647, however, he was accused of anti-Parliamentary activity and imprisoned in the Tower, possibly because of his connection through marriage with the Royalist Earl of Holland. At the Restoration of Charles II in 1660 James was rewarded for his 'inconvenience' by the office of the Privy Seal, with its annual income of £2000. This and other court appointments were not enough to secure the house from further decline, and in 1666 it was agreed that the king, attracted to Audley End by its proximity to the racecourse at Newmarket, would purchase the house. A sum of £50,000 was paid, £20,000 of which was to remain on mortgage. Charles took possession in 1668, though the Earl of Suffolk retained much of the adjoining farmland and continued to reside at Audley End as 'Keeper of the Palace'.

sought her return. He was eventually bought off by George II, who paid him £1200 a year via an allowance to Henrietta. In 1728 Charles and Henrietta were legally separated.

Using the proceeds of a settlement of £11,500 given to her by George II, Henrietta built for herself a grand Palladian villa, Marble Hill House, at Twickenham. This became a well-known meeting place for the leading literary and artistic figures of the day. Henrietta retired from court life in 1732 and in June 1735 married the Hon George Berkeley.

Charles Howard had died in 1733 and was succeeded by his son Henry, the tenth earl. Remarkably, Henry achieved solvency (a status last enjoyed by the first earl before his downfall in 1618), largely as a result of a dowry of £25,000 arising from his marriage to Sarah Inwen, the daughter of a wealthy brewer. The house benefited from this injection of funds and a number of improvements were undertaken, despite £18,000 being consumed by the earl's inherited debts.

government posts, including First Commissioner of Trade and Plantations (the equivalent of today's President of the Board of Trade) and Lord Lieutenant of Essex. It was he who, after consulting the architect Sir John Vanbrugh, ordered the demolition of much of the house.

Both title and property then passed to Charles William Howard, the seventh earl. Charles had served as page of honour at the coronation of George I. He succeeded his father to the post of Lord Lieutenant of Essex and seemed destined for high office until his untimely death in 1722 at the age of 29. Thereafter the property and title were split, for, having no children, Charles William left the estate to his younger uncle Charles Howard, while the title passed to his elder uncle, Edward. The eighth earl was described as having 'great inclinations to versify and some derangement of his intellect'. He mounted an unsuccessful legal challenge to the settlement but the house remained with Charles, who, on his brother's death in 1731, became the ninth Earl of Suffolk.

The ninth earl was described by the eighteenth-century diarist and courtier Lord Hervey as 'wrong-headed, ill-tempered, obstinate, drunken, extravagant [and] brutal'. His wife, however, was a woman of some renown. Henrietta Hobart, daughter of Sir Henry Hobart of Blickling Hall, Norfolk and Woman of the Queen's Bedchamber, famously became the mistress of the Prince of Wales, later George II. She was on poor terms with her husband, not least over the parlous state of their finances, and finally left him in 1717. A long and bitter struggle ensued while Charles

A NEW ERA: ELIZABETH, COUNTESS OF PORTSMOUTH

Henry was to be the last Suffolk earl to reside at Audley End; following his death without children in 1745 there ensued a protracted legal wrangle over the rightful beneficiaries of his estate. The dispute was finally resolved in 1747 when the property was subdivided between a number of recipients, two of whom were grand-daughters of James, third Earl of Suffolk: Elizabeth, Countess of Portsmouth (1691–1762) and her sister Mrs Anne Whitwell. As part of their share of the estate the sisters received valuable agricultural land to the east of the house, while the house itself passed to a different branch of the Howard family. In 1751, however, Lady Portsmouth purchased the house and its immediate parkland, and immediately undertook a range of improvements to secure the fabric of the building and improve its standard of accommodation.

Elizabeth was a forceful character who was willing to go to great lengths to ensure the continuation of her family name. Her first marriage to Henry Grey ended in widowhood, and in 1741 she married John Wallop, Viscount Lymington (created Earl of Portsmouth in 1743). Henry Grey had left Elizabeth a considerable estate at Billingbear in Berkshire after he had changed his will in her favour. The original beneficiary, Henry's nephew Richard Aldworth, was to inherit the property on Elizabeth's death, provided he assume the family name and arms of Neville (Henry Grey's own family name).

FAR LEFT *Elizabeth, Countess of Portsmouth. According to the antiquary William Cole, she was 'as proud as Lucifer; no German princess could exceed her'*

LEFT *Anne Whitwell, Sir John's mother, was described as kind-hearted and loving, in contrast to her sister Elizabeth*

Having secured the fabric of Audley End, Elizabeth was now determined to provide both for the long-term survival of the estate and the continuation of her own family name of Griffin. In pursuit of this aim she bequeathed the estate to her nephew, John Griffin Whitwell, on condition that he assume the arms and name of Griffin. In 1749 John changed his name by Act of Parliament to Griffin Griffin. Richard Aldworth similarly complied with the terms of his inheritance, so that on the death of Lady Portsmouth in August 1762 both John and Richard inherited their respective estates of Audley End and Billingbear.

A FORMIDABLE STEWARD: SIR JOHN GRIFFIN GRIFFIN

John Griffin Whitwell (1719–1797) was born at Oundle, Northamptonshire and educated at Winchester School. In 1744 he obtained a commission in the Third Regiment of Foot Guards and served against the French army in Flanders until peace was declared in 1748. By 1762 when he inherited Audley End, he had been made a Knight of the Bath, had risen to the rank of lieutenant general and was Member of Parliament for Andover. As a result of injuries received at the Battle of Campen in Germany, Sir John had effectively retired from active military service. Now aged forty-three, he turned his attention to the renewal of his ancestral home.

The cost of the renewal, spread over some thirty years, amounted to over £100,000 – half the cost of the original house. A further £200,000 was spent on running the estate during the same period. To finance this work and the running costs, Sir John was largely dependent on the rents paid by the numerous tenant farmers who worked his estates, which averaged about £3,750 a year. In addition, his residual military duties earned him an average of about £750 a year, while his east coast lighthouse (inherited from Lady Portsmouth) brought in a further £3000 a year through tariffs paid by passing

BELOW *Sir John's first wife, Anna Maria Schutz, daughter of Baron Schutz of Sion Hill, Middlesex. They were married in 1749*

ABOVE *Sir John Griffin Griffin, painted by Benjamin West. Sir John is wearing his general's uniform and sits in a military tent*

RIGHT *Sir John's second wife, Katherine Clayton of Harleyford, Buckinghamshire was only eighteen when she married Sir John in 1765. He was forty-six*

Audley End. The scheme not only threatened the appearance of the Audley End estate but represented a challenge to Sir John's authority, since it was supported by the people of Saffron Walden. Sir John – now Lord Howard – showed generosity in 1794 when harvest failures and increased corn prices brought some local families close to starvation. In order to secure scarce corn supplies he subsidised payments above the market price. He also intervened when potato prices soared, purchasing 30,000 bushels for distribution amongst the poorest families of the neighbourhood.

Lord Howard died in May 1797 and was interred in the family vaults of St Mary's Church, Saffron Walden. The funeral procession was led by Greeton, the chaplain who had officiated daily in Lord Howard's private chapel. Lord Howard had no children and Audley End therefore passed to Richard Aldworth Neville, son of the Countess of Portsmouth's heir at Billingbear. Although they were only third cousins, Lord Howard had ensured that Richard would also inherit the barony of Braybrooke. A condition of his inheritance, as stipulated by the Countess of Portsmouth, was that he and his successors assume the name and arms of Griffin.

Richard expressed a reluctance to take up residence at Audley End as this would necessitate the departure of Lord Howard's widow. Lady Howard, however, reassured him that although Audley End had 'afforded her undescribable happiness for thirty-two years, its principal charm is gone', and that 'the best return you can make me is living in this place with comfort to yourself and affectionate recollections of those who have inhabited it with so much delight for such a number of years'. With the arrival of the Nevilles a new chapter in the history of the house began.

ships. In 1765, following the death of his first wife, Sir John married Katherine Clayton; the dowries from his two marriages brought him £35,000, while a number of inheritances brought further amounts. Though Sir John was not amongst the wealthiest of peers, his annual income by the time of his death in 1797 had risen to about £10,000 a year.

Having embarked on the renewal of his family home, Sir John sought to enhance his prestige by petitioning for the reinstatement of the title of Lord Howard de Walden, last held by his great-grandfather, James, third Earl of Suffolk. He successfully petitioned the king via the Prime Minister William Pitt, and was granted the barony in 1784. In 1788 he was further ennobled when he was created first Baron Braybrooke.

Described as a man of 'piety, humanity and charity', Sir John was also outspoken, determined and single-minded. In 1780 he successfully countered a parliamentary Bill which would have sanctioned the building of a new canal close to

RICHARD, SECOND LORD BRAYBROOKE

In 1780 the second Lord Braybrooke (1750–1825) married Catherine Grenville, sister of the first Marquess of Buckingham of Stowe. Like numerous previous owners of Audley End he was appointed Lord Lieutenant of Essex. He continued Lord Howard's tradition of local good works, endowing a national boys' school in 1815, and supporting the building of the canal previously opposed by Lord Howard (although the scheme was eventually abandoned as a result of the arrival of the railways).

Lord and Lady Braybrooke had eight children. One of their sons, Henry, a captain in the Fourteenth Dragoons, died in Spain at the Battle of Talavera (1809); he was the first of a succession of Nevilles to lose their lives fighting for their country. In 1819 their eldest son Richard married Lady Jane Cornwallis, daughter of the second Marquess Cornwallis, and in the following year they moved to Audley End, while the second lord retired to Billingbear.

A ROMANTIC ANTIQUARIAN: THE THIRD LORD BRAYBROOKE

The third Lord Braybrooke (1783–1858) was a Member of Parliament, a scholar and antiquarian, president of a number of learned societies and a keen sportsman. He and Lady Braybrooke devoted much of their energy to the house they had inherited, with a particular emphasis on restoring its Jacobean ambience. In pursuit of this aim in 1829 they embarked on a grand tour of Europe, visiting great houses and palaces in Germany and Holland. In Antwerp they purchased items of furniture to complement the possessions they already held at Audley End.

In 1823 the scholarly third lord edited the first edition of Pepys's *Diaries*, and in 1836 he published his own *History of Audley End and Saffron Walden*. His other great interest was horse-racing and a number of famous racehorses were bred in the Audley End stables, including Sir Joshua, for which the third lord was once offered £10,000.

In 1854 two of Lord Braybrooke's sons died within a week of each other as a result of wounds received during the Crimean War. Henry, a captain in the Grenadier Guards, was mortally wounded at Sevastopol and his younger brother Grey, an officer in the Fifth Dragoons, was fatally wounded at Balaclava.

The third lord himself died in 1858 and was succeeded by his eldest son Richard Cornwallis, who survived his father by only three years. The

fourth lord, like his father, was a man of learning, particularly in the field of archaeology. He conducted a number of excavations at the nearby Roman Fort and Villa of Chesterford, excavated long barrows in the vicinity, and discovered Saxon weapons at Little Wilbraham, Cambridgeshire. He was also largely responsible for assembling the impressive natural history collection which can still be seen at Audley End. Significantly, in an act of family pride, he took the decision to relinquish the name Griffin and reinstate the Neville name and arms. He was married to Lady Charlotte Toler, but had no male heirs.

ABOVE *Richard Neville, later second Lord Braybrooke, pictured with a spaniel in his arms during his Grand Tour visit to Rome, 1773–74. He is accompanied by other young English 'milordi' and the well-known cicerone and guide, Mr Byres*

BELOW LEFT *Richard, third Lord Braybrooke as a young man*

BELOW *The Audley End stablemaster and horses, with the stables in the background, in a mid-nineteenth-century photograph*

The fate of Audley End in the first half of the twentieth century mirrors that of many aristocratic country houses in England. The collapse of the agricultural economy caused a disastrous fall in land prices and rents, forcing many families to dispose of their great houses. Billingbear was demolished in 1926 and from 1904–14 Audley End was rented out. The tenant was, appropriately enough, Lord Howard de Walden, during whose occupancy the house enjoyed an Edwardian swansong in the great age of country house entertaining. After the lease had expired the seventh Lord Braybrooke returned to his ancestral home with his wife Dorothy and their young family.

The seventh lord died in March 1941. Within three weeks the house had been requisitioned for war use and Lady Braybrooke and her daughter were required to move elsewhere. Both Lady Braybrooke's sons lost their lives in the war: the youngest, Robert George Latimer, Ordinary Seaman, was killed in action in 1941 and two years later Richard, the eighth lord, a lieutenant in the Third Battalion Grenadier Guards, died in action in Tunisia.

The fourth lord died in 1861 and was succeeded by his brother Charles, whose chief interests were agriculture and cricket. He was responsible for laying out the pitch in front of the house in 1842. Charles was succeeded in 1902 by his younger brother, the Hon Reverend Latimer Neville (then aged seventy-five), who was Master of Magdalene College, Cambridge – the college that had been refounded by Sir Thomas Audley in the sixteenth century.

TOP *Mid-Victorian family group outside the State Bedroom. The enclosed arcade gave access directly into the garden*

ABOVE *'Lemon Leaf 4th', a pedigree cow from the herd established by Charles, fifth Lord Braybrooke*

RIGHT *Late nineteenth-century photograph of the house from the south-east, with the parterre or formal flower garden in the foreground*

The house and title now passed to the eighth lord's cousin, Henry Seymour Neville. By this time, however, Audley End was being used by the Polish section of the Special Operations Executive, an organisation so secret that Lord Braybrooke himself was forbidden entry. Before the end of the war Lord Braybrooke began to consider the problem of Audley End's future. He consulted the National Trust's representative, James Lees-Milne, who recorded in his diary a visit to Audley End in June 1944 in the company of Lord and Lady Braybrooke. After some difficulty they gained entry to the house and had 'an excellent picnic luncheon' at one of the garden temples. Initial attempts by the Earl of Wilton to purchase the house came to nothing but Lees-Milne eventually negotiated its purchase for the nation from the National Land Fund for the sum of £30,000.

WARTIME AUDLEY END

During the Second World War Audley End was occupied by the British army. The soldiers were from Bedfordshire, Hertfordshire and Essex regiments, posted on general duty because they were medically unfit for action or had been previously wounded. They were responsible for maintaining the security of the house and estate for the duration of the war.

Corporal Peter Howe remembers: 'Stoking the boilers [at the back of the Lower Gallery] was not a popular job. One felt very vulnerable in the dead of night. There was always the thought at the back of one's mind that the Germans might be sent to knock out the unit ... and this would be their chance to remove the soldiers on guard duty.'

On one particular occasion Corporal Howe recalls how 'Several Brits, I included, in full uniform, returning from a day's leave in London, took an unscheduled ducking when we overloaded the big work-punt, by the road bridge, and it slowly but inexorably sank beneath the waves.'

During the time that the Polish section of the Special Operations Executive had its training centre at Audley End the British soldiers lived alongside their Polish colleagues. Corporal Howe commented that 'although the townspeople were officially ignorant of the base's activities, they must have wondered at the civilian-dressed people in the dead of night moving round the fields'. Some of the Polish soldiers established more permanent links in the area. 'A Lieutenant-Instructor married a Scots girl, and was allowed to take a house in the Little Chesterford area' and a Sergeant-Instructor married an Irish nurse from Saffron Walden Hospital.

One or two civilians continued to live at Audley End throughout the war. 'They would keep an eye on the army, and report any problems to Lady Braybrooke, who would then take it up with the CO. Lady B lived at Littlebury, and would cycle over once a week.'

THE SPECIAL OPERATIONS EXECUTIVE

For over two years, from May 1942 to August 1944, Audley End served as a secret training station for Polish soldiers, mostly officers, who volunteered to be dropped by parachute into German-occupied Poland to serve in the Polish underground movement. This was part of a scheme conceived by Winston Churchill after the fall of France in mid-1940 to foster resistance throughout German-occupied Europe. The Special Operations Executive (SOE) consisted of a number of national sections, Poland being the most distant of the countries represented. This meant a flight of some 2000 miles both ways over enemy territory in a single night between dusk and dawn; such operations were possible only in the course of long winter nights.

The Polish section had a training centre at Audley End. Candidates were trained in various subjects ranging from guerrilla tactics, sabotage techniques and handling explosives, to radio communications and marksmanship. This was followed by a briefing course in which the candidate was informed of the exact conditions in occupied Poland at the time, and given help in working out an individual cover story to enable him to survive. The work was extremely dangerous: of the 316 agents (including one woman) eventually dropped into Poland, over one-third were killed in action or died, often under torture, in German concentration camps.

The interior of the house was well protected against the activity of its temporary occupants. Only one entrance was used and a partition was erected to close the main staircase. Only commanding officers were allocated rooms on the first floor, while the rest of the staff and candidates slept on the second floor. Other rooms were used as examination rooms, and one for making documents the agents would use when they landed in Poland. The outbuildings were turned into clothing and food stores, and tailors' and shoemakers' workshops. The wagon shed was used as a garage and for lessons on explosives.

By the middle of 1944 most operations had been transferred to newly liberated southern Italy which provided shorter and safer routes to Poland. Today the only visible sign of this wartime episode in Audley End's history is the impressive monument near the main drive commemorating the 108 volunteers who paid with their lives for their part in the venture.

ABOVE *Memorial to the Polish soldiers of the Special Operations Executive who perished during the Second World War. The urn was unveiled in 1983 by the Secretary of State for Defence*

AN ARCHITECTURAL
HISTORY OF AUDLEY END

THE ABBEY OF
ST MARY AND
ST JAMES OF WALDEN

The present house was built on the site of the Benedictine Priory of St Mary and St James, founded in about 1140. From humble beginnings it grew to immense proportions. By 1250 a timber chapel and cloister range had been replaced with great stone buildings in the Decorated Style. The abbey church occupied the site of the present north range of the house while a dormitory, refectory, and abbot's lodging stood where the east, south and west ranges were later built. Thus the abbey buildings defined the position and basic ground plan of the house in all its later forms.

FOUNDATIONS
FOR SUCCESS:
THE TUDOR HOUSE

Soon after acquiring the former abbey and its lands in 1538 Thomas Audley set about creating a residence within the lofty stone ranges of the existing building. Much of the church was demolished but the massive nave was retained and three floors inserted into it. The cloister buildings, alleys and garth (courtyard) were retained, and a Great Hall was established within the former abbot's lodging in the west range, occupying the same position as the Hall in the later Jacobean house. The resulting residence, which Audley described in his will as his 'chiefe and capitol mansion house at Walden', would serve his successors throughout the remainder of the sixteenth century.

BUILDING
ON SUCCESS:
THOMAS HOWARD'S
JACOBEAN PALACE

Audley's grandson Thomas Howard, who had inherited the house in about 1582, was a wealthy man who anticipated a long and prosperous career in affairs of state. Crucial to the winning of lucrative government and royal appointments was the ability to provide suitable accommodation for the king and queen and their entourage when they visited. This capacity to accommodate the monarch was the defining characteristic of the great Jacobean 'prodigy' houses; other examples are Hatfield House in Essex and Bramshill in Hampshire. Even by the standards of the time Thomas's palatial new house,

BELOW Audley End by Henry Winstanley. The outer court to the left and the chapel to the right were demolished in the early eighteenth century. The Long Gallery (the cupola of which can be seen on the right) was demolished by the Countess of Portsmouth

LEFT *Hatfield House, Hertfordshire, built for another of James I's ministers, Robert Cecil. Instead of the double courtyard plan it was of a compact E-plan, and was built in brick rather than the more expensive stone used at Audley End*

three times the size of the present Audley End, was exceptionally ambitious. Work commenced in about 1603 and the building was largely complete by 1614. It is reputed to have cost £200,000, a vast sum when compared, for example, with the £12,000 spent on Hatfield House, built in 1607 for another of James's great ministers, Robert Cecil.

The palace was built in two stages, the first comprising the four ranges round the inner court. In effect, the Tudor house was rebuilt, beginning with the west (Hall) range. This phase also included a Chapel, Council Chamber and Great Kitchen (which have since been demolished). The result was a house that was more or less complete in itself. While the internal planning reflected conventions dating back to the Middle Ages, the exterior showed an attention to classical symmetry which was relatively new. For example, the courtyard and the dominant position of the Hall were essentially medieval features, and the windows, with their height, size and emphasised verticals, were reminiscent of late Gothic architecture. However, unlike the earlier house, the new palace was perfectly symmetrical, with the important rooms and correspondingly large windows facing outwards rather than into the courtyard, following the trend set by great houses of the late sixteenth century. The second phase was the addition of the large outer court. These outer ranges were more highly decorated than those around the inner court. The general form and many of the details may have been inspired by French architecture of the late sixteenth century.

A theme which runs through the design of the house is the use in a romantic or symbolic fashion of architectural features originally associated with fortifications, to express a nostalgic link with the medieval age of chivalry. Most notable is the profusion of small turrets, each with a weathervane in the form of a pennant. These formed a stylistic link between the two courtyards.

If the external grandeur of the house reflected Thomas's ambitions for royal patronage, then this was reinforced by its internal planning. This was dictated almost entirely by the needs of a visiting royal household, with the State Apartments on the first floor of the inner court, the family apartments on the ground floor below, and lodgings for the household and servants on the second floor or in the outer court. The house was entered by way of

BELOW *The 'Palace of Audlyene' from the west by Henry Winstanley, c.1676. The occupants of the carriage in the foreground would have disembarked at the main gate and walked through the outer court to the entrance porch of the house*

ABOVE *No illustration of the Jacobean State Apartments at Audley End survives, but this painting of Charles I and his queen dining at Whitehall Palace, surrounded by a throng of attendants and onlookers, gives some impression of how such apartments were used*

two porches, the one to the south for the king, the one to the north for the queen. The tympana over the doorways carry appropriate symbols of peace (for the queen) and war (for the king).

These entrances led into the Great Hall. Except on rare occasions, only servants would have eaten here, with the steward presiding at the high table on the dais. The earl would normally eat in a separate parlour. In the south range was the earl's private suite, consisting of a withdrawing room, bedchamber and closet. The matching suite in the north range would have been the countess's private apartment. Aristocratic marriages were essentially diplomatic alliances; such formal separation would be usual.

Royal marriages, similarly, were political alliances, so that the State Apartments were required to be separate and almost equally grand. Although they were virtually identical in layout, however, there are some differences in the grandness of the approach and the degree of decoration, now reflected only in the surviving modelled plaster ceilings. The south apartment overlooked the Mount Garden, had the finest

ceilings and was intended to be approached via the Great Staircase opening from the dais end of the Hall (in fact this staircase was never built, and the South Stairs may have been used instead). The north apartment overlooked the Cellar Garden and Wilderness and was approached from the screens passage by one of the four corner stairs, which lacked the grandeur of the intended Great Staircase. The Long Gallery linked the two apartments and gave access to the Council Chamber and the Chapel. The Gallery was particularly admired by Roger North, who in *Of Building* (*c*.1695) wrote:

> I think it is a great complement to a gallery to
> have some breaks, in the nature of bow-windoes,
> not such as are Gothick, and used in old houses,
> but squares setting out one large in the midle, and
> the others at each end some what less. And if great
> curtaines are hung in the strait range, and drawne
> up with great bobbs, it hath a strange aspect of
> grandure. But this supposeth the state of a prince,
> whereof I know but one compleat example,
> and that is Audley-Inn.

Each of the State Apartments appears to have consisted of a Great Chamber, in which meals would have been taken on grand occasions; a Lobby, leading to the Withdrawing Chamber; a Bedchamber and a Closet. All faced outwards towards the gardens. The rooms that faced into the courtyard probably served as a dressing room and servants' room (with access to the backstairs). On grand occasions when royalty or other high-ranking guests were not present Thomas Howard would probably have used one of these apartments himself. Both suites seem to have had access to galleries overlooking the Hall from opposite ends, a reflection of another feature of the Great Hall, as a place in which entertainments might be performed.

The addition of the outer court produced not only further lodgings, probably only fully used during royal visits, but also what was virtually a house within a house, centred on the north-west pavilion. Accommodation included a Little Hall, Little Kitchen and probably a Little Gallery and Nursery on the first floor. This complex is likely to have provided less formal accommodation for the earl and countess, and after 1668 was the lodging of the Earls of Suffolk as Keepers of the Palace.

An impression of the impact which the house made on contemporary observers, and the style in which the Suffolks lived, is gained from this account written in 1629–30 by a Dutchman, Abram Booth:

> This house, belonging to the Earl of Suffolk, is such a magnificent building and so splendidly furnished that it excels all the Royal residences with the exception of Hampton Court and Windsor. It is completely built of a very pure white ashlar, provided with beautiful galleries, dining rooms, chambers, parlours and [other] rooms, and these furnished wonderfully well with tapestries and skilful paintings. Amongst others there is a magnificent gallery which is more than a hundred yards long and fifteen wide.

'WE HAVE TAKEN A LIKING TO AUDLEY END...'

The king's decision to purchase Audley End in 1666 must have been influenced by the fact that it required little modification to turn it into a royal palace. In 1688 the Office of Works carried out an inspection and announced that some £10,000 was required for repairs, although only £500 a year was set aside for their implementation.

In the sixty years since the building of the house, state apartments had become more complex. Only selected people were allowed access to the

monarch, and the higher their rank the further they penetrated along the axis of honour, into the apartment. By the time Charles II acquired the house, the number of rooms along this axis had increased, making it necessary to bring the former dressing room into the arrangement. The new sequence was Presence Chamber, Lobby, Privy Chamber, Withdrawing Chamber, Bedchamber and Closet. In 1668 there was only a 'great void' where the Great Staircase should have been, either because the house was never completed or because replacement was intended. The suite with the grandest approach was therefore, by default, the northern one, and this became the king's apartment, reversing the original intention.

Changes in tastes in architecture led to unfavourable judgements of Audley End at this period. The diarist Samuel Pepys, who had been impressed with the house on his first visit in 1660, was less so when he returned seven years later. He recorded:

> The house indeed do appear very fine, but not so fine as it hath heretofore to me; particularly the ceilings are not so good as I always took them to be, being nothing so well wrought as my Lord Chancellor's (Clarendon House in London) and though the figure of the house without be very extraordinary good, yet the stayrcase is exceeding poor.

Despite some repairs being undertaken the house continued to deteriorate. In 1695 George, fourth Earl of Suffolk, in his role as Keeper of the Palace, wrote to Wren to inform him that 'those last great windes has soe extramly shatered the chimneys ... that it is dangerous to walke either in the Courtyard or in the Garden, great stones falling from them daily'. Wren later recorded that 'the whole lead of the house was very defective, much of the timber was decayed, and the Fabric weake, built after an ill manner rather Gay than substantial'.

AUDLEY END IN DECLINE: THE HOWARDS' RETURN

When the house was relinquished by the Crown and returned to the Earls of Suffolk in 1701 it was still in poor order, and by now very old fashioned in its internal planning, form and style. Changes in the way great households functioned had led to a vast reduction in the numbers of upper members of the household requiring accommodation. By 1708 Henry, later sixth Earl of Suffolk, was 'busy to the Utmost of his force in New Moulding Audley End', with John Vanbrugh (1664–1726), a distant relative, as his architect. This work involved the demolition of the north and south wings of the

outer court, including the servants' lodgings and kitchen. The west range was retained, and the small kitchen within its north pavilion now became the principal kitchen of the house. In order to link this isolated building to the main house a subterranean passage was built, part of which survives today. Vanbrugh is thought to have made other improvements, including the design of the staircase screen in the Great Hall.

Further changes were made in about 1725 during the stewardship of Charles Howard, later ninth Earl of Suffolk; the designs are said to have been provided by Nicholas Dubois, a Huguenot refugee. The west range of the outer court was demolished and replaced with two new pavilions (the northern one of which continued to house a kitchen), linked together by a screen wall. Further work at this time involved the demolition of the Jacobean Council Chamber and Chapel on the east side of the house. A new two-storey chapel, entered from the vestibule, was formed in the original northern Great Chamber and ground-floor rooms below. (The present chapel occupies the site of the upper part of this earlier chapel.)

In 1736 the open arcade along the south front of the house was enclosed and divided up to form three extra rooms – a dining parlour, drawing room and library – for the tenth Earl of Suffolk. This reflected a mid- and late eighteenth-century trend to locate the main rooms of the house on the ground floor, although the earl is said also to have preferred this arrangement because he suffered from gout.

A NEW BEGINNING: ELIZABETH, COUNTESS OF PORTSMOUTH

On the death of the tenth earl serious consideration was given to demolishing the house altogether or to creating a silk manufactory within its shell. However, in 1751 rescue came in the form of the Countess of Portsmouth, whose intervention guaranteed the future of the house. The London architects Phillips and Shakespear recommended a scheme of demolition and adaptation designed to create a more contemporary house plan. Much of the material removed during demolition was sold locally, some of it to a Mr Flowers of Saffron Walden who bought panelling, floorboards and paving. Over 70 tons (tonnes) of lead were removed from the building, selling at a £12 15s 6d a ton. Such sales provided essential funds, both to cover the costs of the purchase of the house and estate, and for repairs to the roof, plasterwork and windows.

The east side of the inner court, occupied by the Long Gallery, was demolished in 1753 and an open arcade created behind the Great Hall to provide a new link between the north and south ranges. Much of the material from the Long Gallery was reused in this process. At the same time the eastern ends of the north and south ranges were reduced in height to one storey. Further work included the demolition of the pavilions designed by Dubois and the creation of a new kitchen in the north wing of the house.

SIR JOHN GRIFFIN GRIFFIN: A GENTLEMAN'S RESIDENCE

In 1762 Sir John Griffin Griffin was the first owner to inherit Audley End in anything like a sound condition. Nevertheless he spent large sums of money on the replacement of much of the poor-quality stone facing (made of locally quarried clunch) with more durable Ketton limestone from Northamptonshire.

Sir John was not only interested in the arts, but also attuned to the world of metropolitan fashion. Within a few months of his aunt's death, he

LEFT Architectural drawing of about 1755 showing Audley End after the demolition of the Long Gallery

BELOW The fashionable architect Robert Adam, in a portrait by George Willison, 1775

summoned Robert Adam (1728–92) and Lancelot 'Capability' Brown (1716–83) to Audley End. They represented the most advanced taste in architecture and landscape gardening of the day and were asked to collaborate in a thorough replanning of house and park. Adam's most notable achievement was a suite of neoclassical reception rooms for fashionable entertaining. By the 1770s Audley End, which had come so near to destruction just a few years before, was re-established as one of the finest houses in the country.

In 1763 the link corridor built for Lady Portsmouth was rebuilt to a wider measure, and a further two storeys were constructed above. This provided communication at all three levels between the north and south ranges. In the same year work began on the service block and kitchen to the north of the house which survive today. Designed by Adam, the new block housed the brewhouse, dairy and bakery, and was screened from view within a walled enclosure. The dairy, a source of aristocratic entertainment besides fulfilling its practical function, was entered from Lady Griffin's garden (now the parterre garden) via a classical portico. The kitchen was linked to the house by means of a corridor to minimise the risk of fire. Here Sir John's

French chef prepared elaborate meals using fresh produce from the extensive kitchen gardens. Around 1770 a laundry was added. The clean laundry was hung to dry on great horses (racks) suspended from the ceiling, or laid out on the lawns in the service yard.

The addition of the new kitchen and service block meant that the service rooms on the ground floor of the north range could be reordered. At the same time the entire range was extensively repaired and decorated throughout. By 1777 the old kitchen had been converted into a servants' hall while the other rooms were being used for estate and house business, presided over by the steward and butler. In the east bay Sir John built a marble bath, which could be reached by a staircase from the private family apartments on the first floor above. These comprised Sir John's dressing room and bedchamber on the north side and Lady Griffin's dressing room and bedchamber on the south.

The ground-floor rooms of the south range were redecorated between 1768 and 1774 following designs by Adam. The redecorated suite comprised an 'Anti Room' or Lobby, Dining Parlour, Great Drawing Room, Little Drawing Room, Library, Water Closet, Sir John's Writing Room and a Supper Parlour.

The Great Hall, the main function of which was now that of grand entrance chamber and staircase, was also extensively repaired. Its timber panelling and seventeenth-century screen were given three coats of white paint to create the appearance of stone. An upper screen of plaster, also painted to emulate stone, was added to Vanbrugh's stone staircase screen at the southern end of the Hall.

At the same time a new chapel was created in the upper half of the earlier two-storey chapel. It was designed and built by the carpenter John Hobcroft in the Gothick style. This was no doubt considered particularly suitable both for its ecclesiastical connotations and because of the Jacobean origins of the house.

LORD HOWARD DE WALDEN: A NOBLEMAN'S SEAT

Sir John's elevation to the peerage in 1784 inspired a further series of changes. Audley End now had to fulfil the much grander role of nobleman's seat. A further impetus was provided in 1786, when the remote possibility of receiving King George III became an apparent certainty. Although this visit never took place because of the king's illness, the summer of 1786 was a period of intense activity at Audley End.

The principal change was the creation of a new State Apartment, sumptuously appointed for the reception of the king, in the south wing. This was approached from the Saloon and reinstated the original processional route from the Great Hall up the Great Staircase. To provide more accommodation Lord Howard raised the single-storey bays at the ends of the north and south ranges by two storeys.

The Saloon was completely redecorated to serve as a grand reception room. Here guests could congregate before dinner, descending the south staircase to enter the new Dining Parlour below. By the late eighteenth century dinner would have been

served at about four o'clock in the afternoon. When it was over the ladies would withdraw to the Little Drawing Room leaving the gentlemen to talk and drink in the Dining Room. Eventually the groups might reunite either in the Great Drawing Room or the Library for tea or coffee. On less formal occasions guests may have circulated through the ground-floor rooms, dancing, talking or playing cards before taking supper in the Supper Parlour.

THE SECOND LORD BRAYBROOKE

Lord Howard's heir in 1797 was Richard Neville, second Lord Braybrooke. With characteristic tact he refrained from making any changes inside the house until after Lady Howard's death in 1809. Thereafter, his modifications were minor and dictated by practical concerns: larger book-cases for the Library and the conversion of the North Parlours into informal sitting rooms.

In 1819 the royal visit for which Lord and Lady Howard had made such careful preparations took

ABOVE *The south-east elevation after 1786 (compare this with the drawing on page 43)*

BELOW *Elevation of the east wall of the Saloon by Placido Columbani showing the arrangement of the family portraits, c.1786*

place. The Duke of Gloucester and his wife Princess Mary, accompanied by the Duke's sister Princess Sophia, stayed at Audley End for a few days on their way back from Cambridge. Although the etiquette was much simpler than it would have been in the 1780s, the visit was conducted with great splendour. The house was filled to capacity and thirty-seven people sat down to dinner in the newly adapted Dining Parlour.

THE THIRD LORD BRAYBROOKE

Between 1825 and 1835 the third Lord and Lady Braybrooke carried out a series of alterations that were almost as extensive as those of Lord Howard. There were many reasons for these changes, from essential running repairs and practical provisions such as nurseries for their eight children, to wider considerations of fashion and propriety. As he discovered more about the magnificence of the

Suffolks' palace, the third lord realised the outstanding place Audley End occupied in the history of English architecture. In 1836 his studies culminated in the publication of a *History of Audley End and Saffron Walden*. While revering, and seeking to emulate, Jacobean architecture and decoration, he unhesitatingly condemned Lord Howard's approach, reserving particular contempt for the Gothick chapel, 'its mode of decoration sufficiently objectionable under any circumstances, but perhaps never adopted with less judgement or worse effect'.

Lord Braybrooke employed the architect Henry Harrison to help him purge the house of its neoclassical decorations and re-stress its Jacobean character. (In the event, however, many of his ambitions were scaled down, leaving substantial portions of Lord Howard's work intact.) The internal planning of the house was extensively reorganised, particularly in the south wing, where the principal entertaining rooms were re-established

BELOW *Henry Shaw's design for the Great Hall, c.1820, featuring Jacobean revival furniture. The design was never executed*

on the first floor – as they had been in the seventeenth century. A new dining room, two libraries and a drawing room were created in the space formerly occupied by Lord Howard's State Bedroom apartments, while, conversely, Adam's apartments on the ground floor were subdivided to provide replacement bedrooms. Adam's Library, the ceiling of which had projected above first-floor level, was subdivided into three rooms and the ceiling destroyed in order to give an even floor level above. Few structural changes were undertaken in the remainder of the house though all the rooms were redecorated.

Once he had taken the decision to make Audley End his principal home, Lord Braybrooke moved the most important treasures and relics from the former family seat at Billingbear and incorporated them in his new arrangement. These included portraits, furniture, pictures and a library. Similarly heirlooms inherited by Lady Braybrooke from her father, the second Marquess Cornwallis, found new homes at Audley End.

Through the arrangement of these inherited items, together with new purchases and modifications to the house itself, Lord and Braybrooke imposed their distinctive character on Audley End. It is their taste that is stamped on the house today, the rooms arranged and decorated much as they left them. A more complete idea of their work can be gained by reading the tour section of this guidebook.

AUDLEY END
AFTER 1858

The third lord's descendants made no major changes to Audley End. Significant repairs were undertaken by the fifth lord, who also formed the Lower Gallery in 1863 by glazing in the open portico on the east front. The lease of the house to Lord Howard de Walden in the years leading up to the First World War was a short one, so the interiors did not undergo modernisation.

In 1916 the remaining contents from Billingbear were brought to Audley End, adding a further layer to its richly furnished rooms. The seventh lord and his wife carefully preserved the house and its historic contents until the outbreak of the Second World War, when it was requisitioned by the Ministry of Works. The ministry made special arrangements to safeguard the house, placing all the furniture in the State rooms and Chapel where it remained until 1945. At the end of the war the ministry was responsible for restoring the house to its pre-war condition. This entailed unstacking all the furniture and replacing each piece in its proper room, a difficult task in spite of the inventories that had been made.

Audley End passed into the ownership of the nation, under the management of the Ministry of Works, in 1948. In the 1960s the ministry recreated Adam's Dining Parlour and Great Drawing Room, destroying the bedroom apartments created by the third Lord Braybrooke (a decision which would probably not have been taken two or three decades later). Today English Heritage continues to care for this great house through an evolving programme of research, repair and conservation.

LEFT *Design for the ceiling of the third Lord Braybrooke's new Drawing Room, c.1825, based on the Jacobean ceiling in the adjacent South Library*

BELOW *Plan of the south range in about 1835, as remodelled by the third Lord Braybrooke*

THE PICTURE COLLECTION

The picture collection of a country house is not like that of a public art gallery; it was not usually assembled to illustrate the work of schools of art in a didactic manner, nor is each picture an outstanding example of an artist's work. Instead, it is an expression of the personal taste of successive members and generations of a family and their response to the fashions of their time. Such a collection is unique for its historical association with a family and a particular house and for the story of its evolution and survival. It discloses much about the political alliances and public standing of a family, and is closely interwoven with the history of personal relationships and dynastic marriages.

Picture collections of the sixteenth century contained mostly family portraits and portraits of royalty, to the latter of which a family might owe its position of power and social status. Visiting Audley

End in the 1662, William Schellinks saw 'portraits of the ancestors of the Earls of Suffolk, and of many kings, of Henry VII, Henry VIII, James, Charles I, Henry IV of France, Queen Elizabeth and many other kings and nobles.' Samuel Pepys admired a portrait of Henry VIII, who had originally granted Walden Abbey to Thomas Audley. Amidst the turbulent politics and social changes of the Tudor period, old established families symbolically reinforced their claim to eminence by creating ancestral picture galleries. It was a practice that was quickly taken up by the new men of power, such as Thomas Audley. Portraits of successive generations of family members arrayed in the long galleries of late sixteenth- and early seventeenth-century houses testified to a maturing lineage, and provided an edifying example to their descendants.

The picture collection formed at Audley End by the first Earls of Suffolk began to be dispersed after three generations, reflecting the family's declining fortunes. By 1751, when the Countess of Portsmouth became the new owner of Audley End, the house was virtually empty and in a ruinous state.

The collection of paintings assembled at Audley End thereafter was developed through inheritance and marriage, as well as by purchase. Its enduring character was established over three generations by Sir John Griffin Griffin and later by the third Lord Braybrooke. It has changed little since, apart from the addition of new family portraits in the nineteenth century and the arrival of the last pictures from Billingbear (the Neville family seat in Berkshire) in 1916. Its multi-layered character displays the pedigrees of the Howard, Griffin, Grey, Neville and Cornwallis families. In addition, Sir John assembled a collection of 'Old Masters' comprising Italian, Dutch and Flemish paintings, mostly of the seventeenth century.

Sir John Griffin Griffin's ancestral collection began with a nucleus of Griffin family portraits from Dingley Hall, Northamptonshire. These were augmented by portraits left to him by his aunt, the Countess of Portsmouth. Her acquisition of Billingbear following the death of her first husband left her with a collection related to the Neville and Grey families, although this remained mostly at Billingbear in the care of her Neville heirs until the early nineteenth century. In the Picture Gallery at Audley End Sir John hung two views of the Earl of Portsmouth's seat, Hurstbourne Priors in Hampshire, which the earl had commissioned from Jan Griffier the Younger. In a comparable act of patronage, Sir John commissioned William Tomkins to paint six views of Audley End and its gardens.

Sir John's ambition to revive the ancient fortunes and Howard titles of his family directed his ancestral collecting towards the acquisition of portraits of English monarchs past and present, and of members of the Howard family associated with Audley End. Some pictures were given to him by friends, such as the important portrait of Margaret Audley, Duchess of Norfolk, mother of the first

Earl of Suffolk, the builder of Audley End. The portrait was painted by Hans Eworth in 1562.

The making of copies and secondary versions of portraits was an acceptable way of disseminating images amongst friends, relations and political allies, and many images of royalty were copied for courtiers and gentry. In 1786 Sir John bought portraits of King George III and Queen Charlotte to hang, appropriately enough, in his new State Bedroom and adjacent dressing room. The artist was William Hanneman but they were based on Thomas Gainsborough's portraits at Windsor Castle, which had been exhibited at the Royal Academy in 1781.

The real focus of Sir John's ancestral picture collecting was the Saloon. In the 1770s he commissioned Biagio Rebecca to paint a series of Audley, Howard and Griffin family likenesses (all copies or adaptations of earlier portraits), which were fitted into the panelling of the Saloon. A number of Griffin portraits from Dingley were included, their canvases being extended to fit the panelled recesses. The purpose of this cycle was to illustrate Sir John's and his Griffin ancestors' descent – through the Earls of Suffolk – from Thomas Audley. Sir John is portrayed in a formal manner, standing full-length in the ceremonial robes of a Knight of the Order of the Bath.

A further significant strand in Sir John's collecting was the formation of a collection of 'Old Master' paintings. These display the taste of the eighteenth-century connoisseur, comprising Dutch

ABOVE View of the Valkhof at Nijmegen, *1646, by Jan van Goyen. The third Lord Braybrooke visited the scene of the painting in 1829 and commented: 'I have a picture of Schevening by Vlieger still very like'* and Flemish landscapes and maritime pictures, genre scenes, contemporary Italian pictures of landscapes with classical ruins, and seventeenth-century mythological scenes or religious subjects. Sir John hung these in the two North Parlours, the more private rooms in the wing remodelled by Robert Adam. In this context they were treated as 'cabinet' pictures, precious objects inviting private scrutiny.

Whereas Sir John's collecting activities reflect his interest in family genealogy and contemporary connoisseurship, Richard Neville, third Lord Braybrooke, focused on recreating the interiors of the house in a contemporary and romantic vision of the seventeenth century. He inherited not only the picture collection formed by Sir John, but also important portraits and other pictures from the Neville family seat of Billingbear, and portraits from the Cornwallis family brought to Audley End by his wife, Jane Cornwallis. Lord Braybrooke revived the idea of a Jacobean picture gallery, where consecutive generations of a family were displayed in affirmation of the continuation of a way of life from one generation to the next: to this end he hung eighteen Cornwallis portraits in the Picture Gallery built by Sir John. Members of his own family were displayed in the new Dining Room, including the most sumptuous portraits brought from Billingbear, alongside those of similar quality featuring Cornwallis family members.

The third lord treated the Great Hall in a similar manner, hanging it with a dense arrangement of family portraits. The three main strands of the collection are represented. Full-length Cornwallis pictures were hung above the panelling, including the second Viscount Townshend, connected to the Cornwallis family by the marriage of his daughter to the fourth baron. Many of Sir John's ancestral portraits are also seen here, pride of place being given to the Duchess of Norfolk. In the late nineteenth century this precious picture was protected by a curtain, drawn across a rod attached to the picture frame. The Neville portraits brought from Billingbear are mostly of sixteenth- and seventeenth-century family members. There are many portraits of monarchs, including James I, Charles II and William and Mary.

The publication of the third lord's *History of Audley End and Saffron Walden* in 1836 and a separate picture catalogue in 1871 provide a valuable record of the location and manner of display of the third lord's picture collection. Lady Braybrooke's dressing room and morning room was hung with a fine portrait of the Countess of Portsmouth by Thomas Hudson, together with portraits of the second and third Lord Braybrookes. A more personal note was struck by a drawing of the third Lady Braybrooke's mother and a series of portraits of Lord and Lady Braybrooke's children.

Lord Braybrooke selected thirty-six of the Old Master pictures acquired by Sir John to hang in his new Drawing Room. The majority of these were Dutch, partly owing to the contemporary taste for Dutch landscape and genre pictures, and partly perhaps because, apart from the Canaletto view of Venice, these represented the best pictures in Sir John's collection. One of the few contemporary family images in the new reception rooms was a portrait commissioned in 1834 by the third Lord Braybrooke of his wife, Jane Cornwallis. The artist was H W Pickersgill who painted a series of portraits of the Cornwallis family.

Almost as important as the pictures themselves was their decorative effect when hung together. In Lord Braybrooke's Drawing Room they were hung against red flock wallpaper, red being thought to provide the most effective background for pictures of this type, with their rich gilt frames. Although picture rails were installed in other areas of the house according to nineteenth-century fashion, Lord Braybrooke followed the practice of his eighteenth-century predecessors by not using picture chains in the Drawing Room. The small gilt labels on pictures throughout the house bear catalogue numbers referring to the 1871 picture catalogue. Audley End never had picture lights as it had no electricity, even during the final years of the family's occupation. The portraits of George II and Charles Cornwallis above the sideboards at either end of the third lord's Dining Room are fitted with brackets to hold some form of lamp or candle sconce, but this was probably intended to light the plate displayed on one sideboard and assist the serving of food and drink from the other.

Although some paintings have been retained by the family and are not on display, very few have been sold. Six Old Master paintings were sold in 1981, of which one was re-purchased for the house in 1993. This is a fine still life by Pieter Claesz, which now hangs in the Drawing Room. Pictures in the Dining Room, the Great Hall, the Picture Gallery and Lady Braybrooke's Sitting Room are virtually as they were arranged in the nineteenth century.

BELOW Still Life *by Pieter Claesz, another fine Dutch Old Master acquired by Sir John, and recently returned to Audley End*

THE SILVER
COLLECTION

ABOVE *Cup and cover belonging to the Countess of Portsmouth and made by the royal goldsmith Thomas Heming. It is decorated with motifs appropriate to wine and dining*

The term 'family silver' has many resonances. Like other important groups of objects in a country house, such as paintings or furniture, the collection of silver or 'plate' reflects the changing fortunes of the family which owned it, as well as the more general ebb and flow of fashion and personal taste. Plate played an important part in the elaborate dining rituals of the Middle Ages, when it was displayed on sideboards in the Great Hall and other dining areas so that guests could appreciate the wealth of their host. Indeed the wealth of a powerful man was represented by the amount of plate and rich textiles he owned, since both commodities were portable and easily disposable when funds were required. Plate has never quite lost this symbolic significance and still retains an unspoken role as a financial resource and expression of wealth at many levels of society. The ancient custom of displaying plate on a sideboard has survived throughout the centuries.

Plate is usually one of the first assets to be sold when a family falls on hard times. For example, the debts accrued by the Earls of Suffolk, the first owners of Audley End, resulted in a sale of plate in 1640–41. A family collection can also be broken up for inheritance purposes, or, conversely, enhanced through inheritance, marriage and other alliances. The surviving Audley End plate reveals just such a history. It also reflects the changing social position of the Griffin and Neville families as they moved between the upper gentry and the nobility. The items that are now displayed in the Butler's Pantry, and the 'flatware' (cutlery) stored elsewhere, represent only about 12 per cent of the plate listed in the 1881 and 1902 'Inventories of Plate' and can only hint at the overwhelming size and grandeur of the collection that had been amassed at Audley End by the late nineteenth century.

Plate was used to mark important family events, recording periods of high office in the service of one's country or significant dynastic marriages. Most of the Audley End pieces are marked with the coats of arms and monograms of succeeding generations of Griffins and Nevilles or carry dedicatory inscriptions.

The earliest documented piece of Audley End plate is a tankard of about 1670 bearing the arms of Anne Rainsford (1688–1707), the wife of James, second Lord Griffin (1667–1715). The Rainsford arms are set in a lozenge, showing that the bearer

was a spinster, a possible indication that the tankard formed part of her dowry; by contrast a pair of candlesticks bears the full impaled arms of both husband and wife. These pieces were part of the Griffin family inheritance which was subsequently augmented by the Countess of Portsmouth, who added some of the most important pieces.

The Countess of Portsmouth's plate included a continental silver gilt dish and cup, which on formal occasions would have been part of the display of silver gilt on a buffet. The dish is engraved with the monogram 'EP'. A fine set of six gilt candlesticks in rococo style was purchased in 1740 by the Countess of Portsmouth's first husband Henry Grey, from the royal goldsmith George Wickes. It cost the considerable sum of £70 16s. Originally plain silver, the candlesticks were gilded by Sir John in 1786; so too was a pair of large circular salvers made by David Willaume II in 1744, which bear the arms of Katherine Clayton, Sir John's second wife. These enrichments suited Sir John's new position as a member of the peerage, and were probably also part of the preparations he was undertaking for the expected visit of George III.

Other pieces, relating to service undertaken on behalf of the Crown, are engraved with the royal coat of arms and cypher of George III. An inkstand by Thomas Heming is engraved with the date 1762 and commemorates the fact that in that year Richard Neville Neville (father of the second Lord Braybrooke) had accompanied the Duke of Bedford's embassy to France to negotiate the Peace of Paris. The Jewel House Warrant Books contain an entry authorising the issue 'to Richard Neville Neville Esq., His Majesty's Secretary of the Extraordinary Embassy ... the quantity of three hundred Ounces of White plate being the usual allowance on such like occasions'. The custom of granting ambassadors plate from the Jewel House, to uphold the dignity of the monarch and to compensate them for their expenses, continued until the early nineteenth century.

Featuring prominently in the collection is plate used in the dining customs of the eighteenth and nineteenth centuries. Egg cups and a cheese toaster were specialist items reflecting the increasing custom in the eighteenth century of taking less formal meals in private rooms. Breakfast, for example, was only just beginning to gain importance as a meal. Sir John is said to have dined in great splendour, using plate at every meal. Wine and other items were always presented on waiters and salvers, of which there are numerous examples of various sizes, while small oval dishes were made as stands for the sauceboats. Two surviving silver baskets with handles would have been used for the service of bread in the eighteenth century. Similarly certain items in the collection reflect specifically nineteenth-century customs, such as the ice spades (spoons), muffin dishes and cutlery for dessert.

Candelabra were important as decorative items, as well as providing the main source of light for the diners. Chamber candlesticks, of which a number survive, continued in use into the twentieth century. The Hon Mrs Ruck, daughter of the seventh Lord Braybrooke, remembers going up to bed with a candlestick issued to her by the butler.

The Audley End plate also reveals the antiquarian interests of the third lord. A large standing cup in a fanciful seventeenth-century style was made for him in 1831 by Edward Farrel, a specialist in historical revival styles. It is inlaid with coins inherited by the third lord's wife Jane Cornwallis, and bears the following inscription: 'These medals were given to Frederick 1st Lord Cornwallis Comptroller of the Household to Charles IInd as his coronation fee April 23 1661'. Other early pieces, such as a two-handled cup or porringer (1688–89) and a small chalice (*c*.1696), may have been purchased by the third lord to display on his buffet, a 'medieval' ritual which would have appealed to him. An engraving of the Great Hall depicting the wedding celebration of his oldest son in 1852 shows two triangular-shaped buffets lavishly arrayed with plate. Apostle spoons, also of the seventeenth century, had their bowls regilded and were put into practical use as 'Ice Spoons'.

Historical revivals in the early twentieth century were mostly of early and later eighteenth-century styles. A large circular salver with a pie-crust edge and a punch bowl were made in early eighteenth-century style as presentation pieces to the Reverend Latimer Neville, sixth Lord Braybrooke, to mark his jubilee as Master of Magdalene College, Cambridge in 1903.

BELOW *Pair of candle-sticks by George Wickes and dish by David Willaume II, both inherited by Sir John from the Countess of Portsmouth; the dish displays her monogram. Sir John gilded the candlesticks to make them more splendid*

THE NATURAL
HISTORY COLLECTION

Modern-day visitors to Audley End are sometimes bemused by the immense numbers of stuffed birds and other natural history curiosities which crowd the glazed cabinets in the Picture and Lower Galleries of the house. While these tableaux may not be to everyone's taste, the displays – swarms of beady-eyed birds naturalistically mounted in elaborate landscape settings – are certainly impressive and constitute one of the most important ensembles of their kind to survive in any country house. They remind us, moreover, of the consuming passion of the fourth Lord Braybrooke and make a notable contribution to the pronounced mid-Victorian character of the interiors at Audley End.

The natural history collections at Audley End were largely formed by the Hon Richard Neville, born in 1820, the eldest son of the third Lord Braybrooke. As well as being a keen amateur archaeologist young Richard took a precocious interest in natural history and appears to have been encouraged in his hobby by his parents. In 1832 they ordered a cabinet for their son's fossils and when he was 15 he was allowed to install his collection of stuffed birds and animals in a series of glass-fronted cabinets in the Picture Gallery. A watercolour by Lady Emily Townshend shows the display, the cases elegantly mounted on stands with turned legs. Most of Richard's specimens were British birds, shot at Audley End or at neighbouring estates and mounted by professional taxidermists, both local and London firms. Some were gifts from relations and friends. A particularly prized specimen must have been a Greater Bird of Paradise, an exotic curiosity which still bears a label – 'This Bird was presented to King William the Fourth by the King of Oude and was alive in England'. The label goes on to relate how its skin passed into the possession of the king's sister, the Princess Augusta, who gave it to Neville at Frogmore. Other specimens appear to have been originally kept as pets, including a Golden Eagle which 'died in the Audley End Aviary'. The Aviary seems to have been a regular source of specimens for the collection – indeed, it may even have been the origin of the taste for taxidermy at Audley End. As early as 1774 it is recorded that Sir John Griffin Griffin ordered that a Golden Pheasant that had died in the Audley End Menagerie be stuffed and sent up to his house in London.

But it is clear from the scale of his acquisitions and the lengths he went to procure specimens that Richard's collection was more that just a youthful accumulation of natural history oddities. An inventory of the mid-1840s lists no fewer than 99 cases of birds, and five years later these were supplemented by a consignment of 136 exotic natural curiosities, sent on the ship *Unicorn* from Fremantle in Western Australia. The specimens, mainly birds but also mammals and reptiles, were sent as skins, packed flat for transport, and were mounted upon arrival. Further expansion accompanied Richard's succession as fourth Lord Braybrooke in 1858 and it was in this year that he embarked upon an ambitious programme of rearranging and rehousing his collection. The Picture Gallery was lined with huge cases, surmounted by strapwork cresting in the Jacobean taste and fitted with panes of plate glass. These were filled with chiefly British and European birds, remounted in extravagant tableaux simulating various habitats by the taxidermist F Butt of Wigmore Street, London. Victorian taxidermists delighted in devising highly fanciful 'naturalistic' settings, constructed out of peat, papier mâché or plaster of Paris, painted or sprinkled with sand and garnished with dried or artificial foliage, and the cases at Audley End are particularly notable in this respect. Meanwhile, the old cases were refurbished and refitted with plate glass to receive the gaudier plumaged foreign birds mounted by R Leadbeater & Son of Brewer Street, London. It is possible that Leadbeater had supplied the Australian specimens, since in the 1850s the firm maintained a branch in Melbourne, 'engaged in collecting largely in every branch of the singularly interesting natural history of that Colony'. The fourth lord died in 1861 but his exotic cases were eventually installed by his brother Charles, who succeeded him as the fifth Lord Braybrooke, in the Lower Gallery, a ground-floor loggia which he had specially enclosed to receive them.

The fifth lord continued to add to the taxidermy at Audley End, patronising the famous taxidermist John Gould (better known for his lavishly illustrated books on birds) for the purpose, and augmenting the collection with old friends such as 'Paddy', an otter, 'purchased when quite young and tamed by Lord Braybrooke during a fishing expedition in Connemara, August 1867', which 'lived afterwards many years in a pond in the Rose Garden'. It was the fifth lord who, in 1866, compiled a manuscript catalogue of the collection, identifying each specimen by its common and Latin names, supplying additional information about its habitat and provenance. Despite the presence of a serious catalogue the collection never assumed the character of a private museum and a photograph of the Picture Gallery taken in 1891 shows it informally furnished with chairs and occasional tables – as well as a pair of extraordinary firescreens apparently made from squashed swans (which, perhaps not surprisingly, no longer survive). A similar relaxed informality prevailed in the rather more sparsely furnished Lower Gallery and both were clearly intended as comfortable and instructive places to while away wet country house weekends.

Today, changes in fashion and an increased concern about the natural environment makes the Victorian mania for taxidermy as decoration seem strange and unappealing to many visitors. However, the collections at Audley End were amassed in an age when the pursuit of natural history was considered a wholesome hobby and few felt any squeamishness about pressing birds and beasts into the service of interior decoration or personal adornment. After all, hunting trophies in the form of antlers, horns and wild animal heads had long been displayed in country houses and arrangements of 'dried birds' and other natural history specimens were treasured in collectors' cabinets well before the nineteenth century. In the 1770s and '80s the Duchess of Portland amassed a celebrated collection of 'natural and artificial curiosities' at her country retreat, Bulstrode, and in 1802 the Menagerie at Hawkstone boasted 'stuffed birds so nicely resembling nature you can hardly distinguish them from the living ones'. However, little of this early taxidermy survives owing to imperfect techniques of preservation and it was only the introduction of arsenical or 'metallic' soap by the Frenchman Becoeur in 1802 that enabled taxidermists to preserve specimens indefinitely.

52

ABOVE *One of the crowded displays devised by R Leadbeater & Son in the Lower Gallery. This case contains no less than 59 exotically plumaged Australasian birds – presumably those despatched from Fremantle in Western Australia to Richard Neville in 1845*

This galvanised the development of 'artistic taxidermy' – an art which exploited the decorative potential of displays of preserved birds and animals as ornaments for the home – and ensured its great popularity in the nineteenth century.

When Audley End first came into public ownership in 1948 the natural history collection was seen as an aspect of the unfashionable Victorian taste that was gradually being eradicated from the house. Lord Braybrooke's birds were banished and put into storage as a 'conservation hazard', but were reinstated when the process of restoring the interiors began in the late 1970s. Over the next decade the collection was conserved, each specimen and the interiors of the cases being carefully cleaned. Although the colours of many of the birds have faded, the introduction of blinds in the Lower Gallery will alleviate further damage. The natural history displays at Audley End are a remarkable survival, and their return and refurbishment is a striking vindication of the enthusiasms of the fourth Lord Braybrooke and of the Victorian taste for ornamental taxidermy.

FURTHER READING

PRIMARY SOURCES
Essex Record Office, Braybrooke archives (D/DBy, accession 5859 and temporary accession 1974), primarily for post-1752 building history of house
Public Record Office, Works and Lord Chamberlain's accounts, for house as royal palace, 1668–1701
Sir John Soane's Museum, John Thorpe's Book of Architecture; Adam drawings collection

SECONDARY SOURCES
Addison, W, *Audley End* (1953)
Braybrooke, Richard, Lord, *The History of Audley End and Saffron Walden* (1836)
Cornforth, J, 'Victorian views of Audley End', *Country Life*, 8 July 1976
Drury, P J, ' "No other Palace in the Kingdom will compare with it"; The Evolution of Audley End, 1605–1745', *Architectural History* 23 (1980), 1–39
Drury, P J, 'Walden Abbey into Audley End' in *Saffron Walden: Excavations and Research 1972–80* (S R Bassett), CBA Research Report 45 (1982), 94–105
Drury, P J and Gow, I R, *Audley End, Essex*, former English Heritage handbook (1984)
Tipping, H A, 'Audley End', *Country Life* 59 (1926), 872, 916; 60 (1927), 94, 128
Tipping, H A, *English Homes, Period III, Vol II: Late Tudor and Early Stuart 1558–1649* (1927), 239–76
Williams, J D, *Audley End: The Restoration of 1762–97* (1966)